My Time in Atlanta

PUBLISHED BY
OUR WRITTEN LIVES OF HOPE, LLC

PRINTED IN THE U.S.A.

Our Written Lives of Hope provides publishing services to authors in various educational, religious, and human service organizations. For information, visit www.owlofhope.com.

All rights reserved. No part of this publication may be reproduced, stored in a retrieval system, or transmitted in any form or by any means, without the permission of the copyright holders.

Copyright © 2014 S. Green
Layout & Design by Rachael Hartman

Library of Congress Cataloging-in-Publication Data
Green, Shirley, 1947
My Time in Atlanta

Library of Congress Control Number: 2014907600
ISBN: 978-0-9894070-4-5

My Time in Atlanta

S. Green

Published by Our Written Lives of Hope

Contents

The Storybook Girl

The Storybook Girl 17

Part One

Flowers for Mary 22
Flowers for Joseph 26

Flowers of Maryfield
Our Community As It Was In 1991

Flowers of Maryfield 31
Mother Mary Jozefa Kowalewski 31
Sister Mary Eulalia 31
Our Dear Sister Charitas 32
Dear Sister Bernadette 32
Now our darling Sister Emmanuelle 32
Now about our dear Sister Maurice 33
Our Sister Mary Immaculata Collin 33
Sister Mary Clare 34
Is Our Pearl! 34
Sister Mary Elizabeth 34
Our Sister Maria Philippa 35
Our Dear Sister Francis Joseph 36
Sister Mary Regina 36
Our Dear Sister Mary Josefa Chicoine 37
Sweet Sister Margaret Mary 37
Our Dear Sister Mary Peter 38
Sister Mary Denise De Sales 38
Sister Mary Agnes 39
Sister Victoria 39

Sister Josephine 40
Sister Jeanne Marie 40
Sister Philomena 40
Barney 41
Little Joe 41
Our Chaplain, Father Michael Hogan 41
Father Vincent Kowalewski 43
Different Gifts 44
Father John Kowalewski 45
Chris - The Special Child 46
Father John Comny 47
Remembering 48
Father Tom Carroll 48
Father Carroll's Book 50

Part Two
A Unique Description

A Unique Description 52

Part Three
Archbishop Wilton D. Gregory
and Some of his Priests

Archbishop Wilton Gregory 60
Archbishop Gregory's Beautiful Voice 61
The Unforgettable Meeting 62
Three Things 62
Father Joseph Mendes 63
Our Beloved Chaplain 63
Father Juan 67
The Senior Discount 68
The Conversation 70
Father John DeVore 70
Father James Henault 71

July 8, 2011	72
Father Neil Jones	73
Father Neil's Sermons	75
A Beautiful Moment	75
Father Michael Hogan	76
Father John Fallon	77
The Prisoner's Priest	77
Father Sunny Punnakuziyil	78
Father Sunny and the Clock	80

Part Four
Golden Memories of My Dear Parents and My Dear Aunt Martha

O Daddy Dear	85
Sweet Susie	86
Rev. Leroy Holmes	87
Sweet Susie's Children	87
God-Willing	88
August 21, 2010	88
Daddy's Gift	89
Untitled 1	90
Feast Day of St. Francis de Sales	90
Daddy's Gravy	91
Daddy's Saying	91
Untitled 2	92
Precious Time	92
October 24, 2006	94
October 29, 2006	95
First Friday	95
All Saints Day	95
November 1, 2006	96
All Saints Day	96
Mrs. Alma Mills	97
Mrs. Jessie Marzett	98
Mother's Jars!	99

Hats! 99
The Special Angel 100
Ms. Theresa 101
Mother's Squirrel 102
December 27, 2005 103
The Last Time 103
Mother's Silver 104
Only For A Time 105
Tam 107

Martha and Martha and Mary

Martha and Martha and Mary 109

Part Five

Dr. Martin Luther King, Jr. 115
A Calling 116
Equiano 118
In a Decade or Two 118

Part Six
Warm Memories of
Others Who Touched My Life

In the Year of 2010 122
Mr. Mike Grady 122
Truly Special 123
Mr. Grady's Family 123
Mr. Tom Grady 124
The Sacred Heart Bouquet 125
The Thank You Note 126
My Sacristy Angel 127
The Sacristy Helpers 128
Emmanuella's Gift 129

Rafaela	133
Ms. Pecolia Brown	134
The Flower Lady	136
Deacon Mobley's Beautiful Gesture	137
Mary, The Deacon's Wife	139
Mr. Higgens	140
Mr. Higgens' Father	141
Mr. Lancour	142
Mrs. Sybil Lancour's Hobby	143
The Beautiful Ceremony	143
Sunday Best	144
The Family Breakfast	145
The Special Kindness	145
The Candle Lighter	146
Precious Rewards	147
Mr. and Mrs. John Ribblett	148
Kroger's Flower Shop	149
Herman and Zeek	149
Sophia's Cake	151
Mr. Frank Lentini	151
Mrs. Attridge and	153
The Nice Lady	153
My Precious Holy Bible	154
The Hidden Talent	155
Mr. and Mrs. Raymond Ferris	156
Tara	158
A Beautiful Act of Charity	159
Mr. Kevin Henderson	160
Kelon's Joy	161
Mr. and Mrs. Eisenberg	162
Ena Neblett	162
Spending Time with the Lord	163
Helen and Rose	164
Mr. Michael Alexander	166
Margaret's Translation	168
Mr. and Mrs. Kenneth Brockway	169
Kenny's Flowers	169

Mrs. Brockway's Painting 170
The Great Surprise! 171
Emma and Hannah 172
Dr. Charles R. Stearns 173
Dr. Laurence Lesser 175
Saint Thomas Aquinas Church Group 176
Kathy Gestar 178
Charles and Dorothy Revard 178
Sister Elizabeth's Sweet Kindness 179
Mr. and Mrs. Minder 180

In the Year of 2011 .... **181**
Tino 181
Ana Maria Vidarte 183
Sandra Znosko 184
The Special Offer 186
Bear 186
The Little Memento 188
Mr. Angelo Bione 188
Mrs. Debbie Bione 189
Billy and Yoda 190
Sister Sponsa Beltran, O.S.F. 191
Mrs. Edith Locsin 193
Alejandro Henao 194
Alejandro's Wife 194
Mrs. Dorothy Baumgartner 196
Andrew to the Rescue 196
Mr. Frank Gabriel 197
Mother Jane Francis 199
And Her Guardian Angel 199
Marien 201
David 202
Madeleine's Trip 203
Lora 203
Mary Rose, Bernadette, Isabell and Mr. and Mrs. Hannish 204
Aileen's Beautiful Gift 206
Shantel 206

The Little Blue Pumps 208
Mr. and Mrs. Charles Matthews 209
September 17, 2011 210
Birthdays and Mrs. Norma Matthews 211
Mr. Richard Hitchcock 212
Mr. Cannon 213
Lady From Maine 214
Mrs. Hubner 215
Mary Ann Kelly 215
The Sweet Gift 216
Shoo-Fly Pie 217
A-Roo-Ka and Her Children 218
Deacon Evelio Garcia Carreras 218
Family Tradition 220
September 26, 2011 221
September 25, 2011 221
St. Joseph's Feast Day 222

In the Year of 2012 222
Mr. and Mrs. Kevin Doyle 222
Mrs. Doyle's Precious Revelation 223
Mr. Doyle's Two Beautiful Gestures 224
Mr. Doyle's Grandsons 225
Dr. and Mrs. Stephen Brena 226
Dr. Brena's Touching Concern 227
Mrs. Brena's Gracious Help 227
The Birthday Cake 228
Mr. and Mrs. Raymond Holstein 229
The Sweetest Card 229
Jim and Justine 230

In the Year of 2013 231
Mr. and Mrs. Michael Bruyere 231
Mrs. Veronica Bruyere 232
The Wedding Pictures 233
Two Precious Pictures 234
Sarah's Gift 235

Mother Francis de Sales Cassidy 235
Gloria Gilbert 236
A Nice Gift 238
Faithful 239
The Little Visit 240
A Special Custom 241
Mr. Coppinger 242
Mrs. Hamilton and Tom 243
The Birthday Bouquet 244
Mr. Mackin 245
A Beautiful Gift 245
The Nerone's and Their Friends 246
Mrs. Maureen Casey 248
The Parting Picture 249
Gloria Still 249
Still Lake 250
The Special Arrangement 251
Dr. Richard Carlin 252

Part Seven
Sister Sunila and The Coyotes

The Coyotes 256
Sister Sunila's Little Adventurous Plight 258
Sister Sunila 260
Sogi, Susan, Sharon, Stephanie and Little Serene 261
February 7, 2010 262
Her Father's Happiness 263
Mrs. Kulangara 264
Little Serene 264
Little Steven 265
The Beautiful Family 266

Part Eight
Little Stories and Little Little Stories

J.J. and The Coyotes 269
Ring! Ring! 271
The Story of Puff 272
J. J. 273
The Bird Ordeal 274
The Beauty of the Morn 276
The Best Alarm Clock 277
The Flock of Robins 278
Thanksgiving Day 279
Hide and Seek 279
Follow the Leader 280
November 4, 2010 281
The Little Adventure 281
The White Tree 282
A Simple Joy 283
Untitled 283
The Bird and the Chipmunk 283
June 28, 2007 284
Sweet Lady of the Sacristy 284
The Pieta 285
April 3, 2011 286
The Unexpected Gift 287
Rose of Sharon 288

Atlanta's Special Child
My Bonnie Blue 290

Part Nine
The Perfect Gift Dedicated To
The Sacred Heart of Jesus
The Perfect Gift 293

The poems in this book
are true experiences
and incidents of my life

The three poems

The Storybook Girl
Dr. Martin Luther King,
Jr.
My Bonnie Blue

have been excerpted
from my book entitled

<u>A Gift For You</u>

Published by
Brentwood Christian Press
in 1990

July 12, 2010

To all of those
Who crossed my path
And are not mentioned
In this book
May God bless and help you
And guide your lives
And may you one day find
That you are mentioned
In His
Book of Life

A Special Acknowledgement

With deep gratitude
I want to thank
Mrs. Sharon McCusker
For typing out
All these poems for me

May God grant her
A very special blessing
For all her kindness
And generosity
And may He one day
Grant her
A beautiful place in Heaven

The Storybook Girl

The Storybook Girl

I was in the Ladies Lounge
of the Atlanta Airport
when a young girl came in
She looked as though
She had stepped from a storybook page.

She wore a pink dress
that had large flowers all over it
And on her head
A most becoming wide-brimmed hat
From which hair
like golden sunshine
draped over her shoulders and down her back
She looked just beautiful.

As I watched her
I just had to tell her - how pretty she looked
She said - Thank You Ma'am
I am so glad you told me that
For I have just started college
And this is my first trip home
And I really wanted to look nice
But I didn't feel too confident about it
I reassured her
And a smile graced her face.

This made me feel good inside
And brought forth - how little things you do
telling someone they look nice
or to have a nice day
or even just a smile
can be so significant and do wonders
to uplift a heart.

And these little things
whether someone knows about them or not
Each of us can do and make a difference
in others lives.

Part One

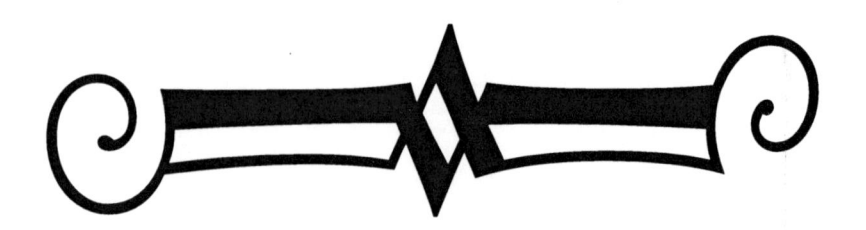

Flowers for Mary

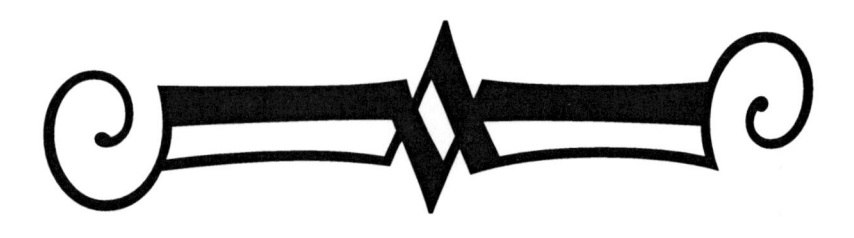

Flowers for Mary

I bring you a lily
that's white as snow
To represent your purity and innocence
From the first moment of your existence

I bring you a sunflower
that's as golden as the sunshine
To represent all the joy
You must have brought your parents -
Saint Joachim and Saint Ann
When you were a child

I bring you gladiolas
To represent your courageous decision
When you said - yes
And became

The Mother of God

I bring you carnations
To represent
Your holy marriage to Saint Joseph

I bring you begonias
To represent your humility
When you went to be of service
to Elizabeth

I bring you primroses
To represent gratitude
For all your daily labors
doing household tasks
And caring for your family

I bring you geraniums
To represent your immediate readiness
to do God's Will

When you left your home
Arrived in Bethlehem
Then finding no room in the Inn
Jesus - The Son of Man
was born in a poor stable

And not only this
But shortly after
You had to take Him
And fly into Egypt for safety
Being exiled from your homeland - for a time

I bring you camellias
To represent the heartache you felt
When you thought Jesus was lost

I bring you poppies
To represent all the kindness, love and care
You showed to those around you

Then I bring you bunches of forget-me-nots
To represent the day
You laid sweet Saint Joseph to rest

I bring you buttercups
To represent all the loving care
You gave to Jesus
While He was growing up

I bring you pansies
To represent thanks
For all you did - to help the Apostles

I bring you tulips
To represent all the prayers for others
You prayed throughout your life

Now I have to give you
Many many bunches of
bleeding hearts
To represent
All you suffered
As you walked close to Jesus
On the way to Calvary

✤

For all the pain you suffered
As you stood
At the foot of the Cross

✤

For all the pain you suffered
As you watched them
Thrust a spear in His side

✤

And then for all the pain
you suffered
As you held Him in your
arms
And then laid Him to rest

✤

And then Dear Mary
I have to give you more
bleeding hearts
To represent
Your heartache
And the silent tears you shed
Every time you thought of it

✤

And now Dear Mother
I bring you many many red
roses
To show my gratitude
For all you have done for me
And all mankind

✤

As I give you this bouquet
Whole and complete
May I one day find it
In the Land
Where the angels came and
took you
As fresh as the day
I first picked it

✤

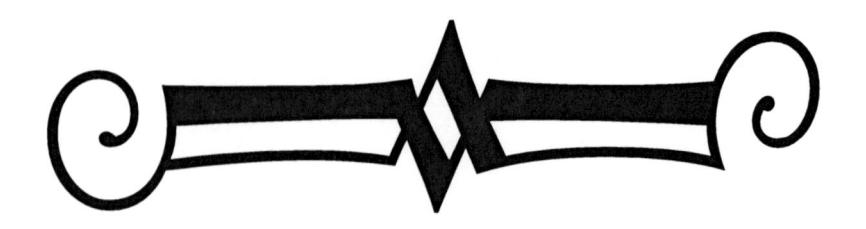

Flowers for Joseph

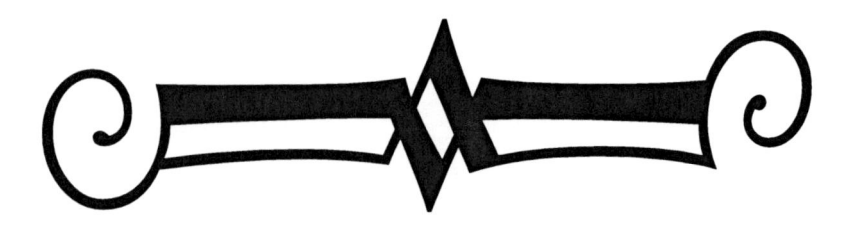

Flowers for Joseph

I give you a lily
For the good and upright life
that you led upon this earth

I give you a lily
for listening to the angel
And taking Mary for your wife

I give you a lily
for the distress you must have felt
on arriving in Bethlehem
And finding no place in the Inn
Jesus - had to be born in a stable!

I give you a bunch of lilies
for your willingness to be Jesus' earthly father

I give you a bunch of lilies
for all the pain and hardships
you suffered
When you had to flee into Egypt
And be in exile, for a time

I give you a bunch of lilies
for all the love and care
you gave to Jesus and Mary

I give you a bunch of lilies
for all your toil and sweat
as you labored hard in your carpenter shop
to support your family

I give you a bunch of lilies
for all the goodness and kindness
that you showed to others

❦

And I give you a bunch of lilies
for my belief
that you accepted death peacefully
as God's will
though Jesus was still young

❦

I give you many many bunches of lilies
for all you have done
to help me and others
through out our lives

❦

I give you
many more bunches of lilies
for those who forget you
or seldom think of you

❦

And I give you
Another bunch of lilies
just to say - I love you

❦

And I pray
My Sweet Joseph
that one day
In a beautiful valley of Paradise
that I will come across
these many bunches of lilies
surrounding the bouquet
I gave Our Lady

❦

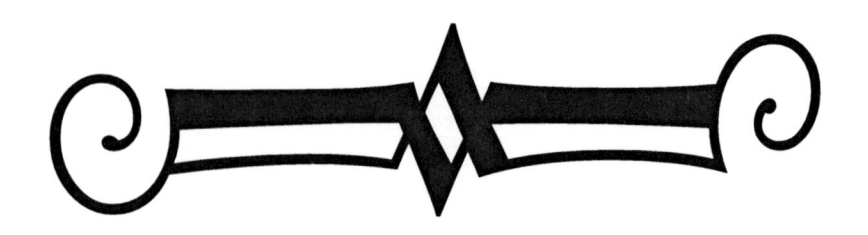

Flowers of Maryfield

Our Community

As It Was

In 1991

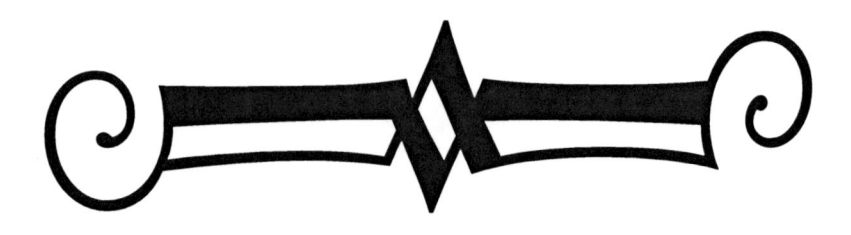

Flowers of Maryfield

The Flowers of Maryfield
Are rare indeed
They are not the kind
that beautify lawns and
gardens
or places along
the highways and byways
Nor do they grow wild
in open fields or along
hidden pathways
and quiet wooded trails

These Flowers of Maryfield
Are flowers
that continually send up
praise
And thanks to God
And witness - His Presence
to the World

By their lives
They try to uplift
And bring hope and joy to
others hearts
And try to help them
experience
A quiet peace - with total
trust in God

These Flowers Are:

Mother Mary Jozefa Kowalewski

Who gives all her
Daughters of Prayer
A special love and care
In both material and
spiritual concerns
And no matter how busy she
may be
She will take whatever time
is necessary
And try to be of help to you
Most of all she does her best
To lead and guide us
Along the right path
So that we may all one day
Come into
The Light of Glory

Sister Mary Eulalia

is the Sister Assistant
Who tells me - many odd
true stories

And when they are funny
we have a good laugh
But all the while my silent
joy

is to watch her face light up
And her cheeks become rosy pink

Besides being the Assistant
she works hard making
beautiful ceramics
And other works of art
She is always busy
And shows us what it
really is to serve the
Lord beautifully in all
circumstances

Our Dear Sister Charitas
Shows us what Fidelity is
She does not get around
As well as she used to
but she faithfully goes
to the sewing room each day
And manages to keep
our clothing well-mended

When she is not doing this
you will find her knitting
or doing some other kind
of needlepoint work
And I tell you - everything
she makes
turns out just beautiful
And so professional looking
that I believe
she could open her own store!

Dear Sister Bernadette
has cooked for the
Community
for many years
Oh! Those delicious meals!
How I love them!
Like Sister Charitas
She doesn't get around
As well as she used to
But what an edification
she is to us for she never
stops going!
She rolls that wheelchair
Right up to the kitchen door
Gets her walker
And enters her domain!

Now our darling Sister Emmanuelle
demonstrates to us in her
illness the virtue
of never complaining

She is so happy with everything
And so very grateful
for anything that's done for her
When she comes to recreation
If you ask her how she's doing
She will tell you -
I am doing fine and dandy
Trying to be sweet as sugar candy!
And she is!

Now about our dear Sister Maurice
What can I say!
She's a character!
She loves to tell us jokes
And keep us laughing all through recreation
And once a year
At Thanksgiving time
She pulls out her old guitar
puts on some funny spectacles
And sings us a bunch of Foolish Questions
Believe me!

Nobody else can do this routine like her

But our dear Sister
does have a serious side
and a special gift
of really being wonderful
with the retreatants
that come here to spend a few days
They love her!
And many keep up with her special days
to send her flowers
or some little gift
Sister Maurice is really
The Community's Charm!

Our Sister Mary Immaculata Collin
is the Mistress of Novices
who try to form us into
Good Visitandines
By teaching us
to follow the rule and directives
of our Holy Founders -
St. Francis de Sales and St. Jane de Chantel
that we may serve God well

She is most gifted in music
And has even written a few songs
She plays the organ for the Community
And never fails to lift her lovely voice
in praising God

⊂━━◆━━⊃

Sister Mary Clare Is Our Pearl!

She is now confined to a wheel chair
And her memory is not what it used to be
But wherever the Community is
Sister Mary Clare is!
She is forever counseling us
To be a Religious!
And not to act like wildcats!
No matter what you say to her
She has a ready reply
And so many remarks
that make you chuckle or laugh outright

Another beautiful thing about her which takes in a most serious matter is the fact
that she continually prays for the dying
She said - It's their last chance!
And she is absolutely right!

How beautiful she must be to God!

⊂━━◆━━⊃

Now our dear and loving Sister Mary Elizabeth

is Sister Mary Clare's buddy
For almost everywhere she is
Sister Mary Clare is too
And if Sister Mary Clare doesn't see her
she wants to know-
Just where is Sister Mary Elizabeth?
They have worked side by side
for many years
And now in the chapel
They pray side by side

Remarkably at 85
Sister Elizabeth
is able to be of tremendous

help
in caring for her precious
friend
She treats her with so much
understanding
and overflowing love and
kindness
It warms my heart so much!
And what an example of
friendship
And overwhelming charity!

A few times
unknown to her
I have observed Sister Mary
Elizabeth
in the chapel alone
in very deep prayer
She seemed to have a
heavenly glow
And I thought
If I could see this from the
outside
Precious! Precious!
She must be
In the sight of God

Our Sister Maria Philippa

I truly believe

has a pair of invisible wings
She can do things so quick
And get from one place to
another
so fast
that I don't think
it's humanly possible!

She too
helps to take care of Sister
Mary Clare
She faithfully wheels her
everywhere she needs to go
And does other special little
things for her
with great love
Sister Mary Clare is her
special joy!
And all the remarks
that Sister Mary Clare
makes to her when they are
alone
gives her a lot of pleasure

Dear Sister Philippa
has a very nice singing voice
and another special gift
of being able to make
beautiful flower
arrangements
And sometimes I tell her
If she was not in Religious

Life
She would make a wonderful Florist

Our Dear Sister Francis Joseph

is one of the carpenters of the Community
I have seen her with hammer and nails, screws and bolts
And whatever else you call those kind of things -
put cabinets and bookshelves together
Then I hear her sometimes talk about other things she can do
down in that carpenter's shop-
A place where you won't find me!

Sister Francis Joseph
is also our bookkeeper
And believe me!
She's not about to let any numbers
get her mixed up and confused!
Besides these two occupations
She is also in charge of Wardrobe
Which includes the task of Habit-making

When I went for a fitting once
I didn't know
I was going to have to stand on top of the table
so she could get the hem - just right!
Sister Francis Joseph believes in being precise
My head nearly touched the ceiling
And it was a great relief - To get down!

She really shows us what determination is
And how to try to do your best
in all your duties!

Sister Mary Regina

is also a carpenter of the

Community
And does absolutely
beautiful work!
I have not met her
because she has been away
for some time
taking care of her dear
Mother
during her illness

We do keep them both in
our prayers
And I know
God will truly give her
A most loving reward
for all that she is doing

⊂━━━◦

Our Dear Sister Mary Josefa Chicoine

is in charge of the Host
Room
She keeps everything
running smoothly
including the people around
her
For her wonderful
disposition
makes working for her a
pleasure

During the Divine Office
She lends her beautiful voice
to the chanting of the
psalms and prayers
And on some special
occasions
or sometimes at Mass
She brings out the zither -
A musical instrument
somewhat like the harp
And as she plays
those heavenly tones almost
lift you to Paradise

From our dear sweet and
kind Sister
We learn generosity
For her generous heart
Almost surrounds the sky!

⊂━━━◦

Sweet Sister Margaret Mary

is our Sacristan
I help her there
And I know how she likes
Everything Just So
She wants all things
to be neat and nice for God
And spends much time
to keep it so

I believe her deep care and concern
must please Him very much

This example
of our dear Sister
helps us to remember
to always keep Him - First
in our lives

Our Dear Sister Mary Peter

is in charge of the Laundry
And she tries to keep
All our clothes nice and clean
Sometimes I see her
make so many trips
up and down those
basement stairs
that I wish
she had a pair of those
invisible wings
like Sister Maria Philippa

At Recreation our dear Sister
may tell a joke or two
But she has her own few words
of special philosophy

that she has to endow us with
Sometimes these few words are wise
And sometimes they are - otherwise
But we all love her
and she helps to brighten the day

Sister Mary Denise De Sales

keeps our grounds looking beautiful
She loves to climb aboard
Big Al - the tractor
And head into open space
Where they seem to enter
their own sphere

And on those days
When Big Al is not feeling well
she knows just what to do
to make him perk up
And feel better
so they can get back on the job!
Now what I find unusual
About Sister Denise

is her great tenderness for
animals
even bugs and those creepy
spiders
If they happen to get into
the building
she scoops them up and
heads outside
before one of her dear Sisters
come along
And takes their life
This great tenderness
does extend to people too
For she spends a lot of time
giving Sister Emmanuelle
excellent care
And she does it with much
love

I am sure God will bless her
for all she does
And will help her watch
after
All her creeping and
crawling friends

Sister Mary Agnes
has a specialty of making
beautiful cards
for different occasions

She seems to be able to find
things in the art closet
that nobody else can find
I am beginning to wonder
if she has a secret hiding
place there

Our dear Sister also knits
well
And has made a number
of lovely items
If we don't watch her and
Sister Charitas
they may decide
to go into business for
themselves

Sister Victoria
is our new postulate
she can lift your spirits
just by watching her
For she always seems to be
bubbling over with joy
And so full of energy
And enthusiasm
to do whatever charge
she is given
Our dear Sister is really a big
help!

Before she entered
she brought us some of her
delicious
Home-made Chocolate
Chip Cookies
So I am sure
there will be more than a
little persuasion
to get her in the kitchen
to make this specialty
from time to time

We love her!
And we sure do love those
cookies too!

And I
Sister Shirley
Am but a fragile flower
Just trying to please and
glorify
The Sacred Heart of Jesus
Who is - The Love of My
Life
Hoping that
When anyone thinks of me
They will think of the Sacred
Heart

And I pray
That one day
We can all be found

In the Glory of Paradise
Blooming eternally
In the Garden of His Heart

⁌━━▲━━⁌

Sister Josephine
Sister Jeanne Marie
Sister Philomena

These three dear Sisters
have recently transferred to
Maryfield
from Parkersburg, Virginia

They were teaching there
but have decided to embark
upon the Monastic Life

We graciously welcome
them
And hope they will be very
happy here
It's only been a short time
since their arrival
But already
They blend right in!

There are two pets at Maryfield

Barney

The snow-white cat
that is treated like a king
by Sister Denise
He really has her wrapped around
his little furry paws!

And then there is the pet dog

Little Joe

Who is Sister Mary Peter's pal
And true friend and companion
He too, has stolen her heart!

Our Chaplain, Father Michael Hogan

Our Chaplain here at Maryfield
is Father Michael Hogan
He truly looks after us
with much love and care

Two days ago was Valentine's Day
It fell on a Sunday
this year of '93
To our surprise Father brought us
one of the sweetest little flower arrangements
you've ever seen
And this past Christmas
he brought each Sister
A precious little gift

This is a glimpse
of the nice little things he does
But far surpassing these
He really cares for our souls

Each morning he gives us
A most serious and enlightening sermon
For he spends much time
in study and reflection
I believe his number 1 source
is the great Doctor of the Church
St. Thomas Aquinas

who truly has captured
a special place in his heart

Sometimes
Father says
He's an old-fashioned priest
because his sermons
are longer than many today
But they are all
so very good and helpful
and we are most grateful to
him

Now often at the end of
Mass
Father likes to tell us
A few more words
or some little joke
to make us smile
So before I close this poem
I would like to say
A few more words

In the Summer of '93
June or July
We had a 7:30 evening Mass
on First Friday
in honor of the Sacred Heart
Father had come for
Benediction at 5:00 pm
And decided to stay in the
parlor area
until Mass time
for he lived 33 miles away
I was handing out programs
to the people as they came
in
I began to become
a little alarmed
for it was almost 7:30
and Father
had not come from the
parlor area
Finally, I went to check
And there was Father Hogan
in great dismay
locked between
the two set of doors
we have in the foyer area!
I couldn't help laughing!

He had to admit
to the congregation later
that he had called on
The Whole Heavenly Host!

That really was some ordeal!
And Father hasn't stayed
over since!

Now that I have said
A few more words
to make you smile
I do hope and pray

that the Sacred Heart
will bless Father Hogan
Immensely in this life
And one day bring him
home
to rest eternally
on His Heart

⊙━━◆━━⊙

Father Vincent Kowalewski
August 7, 2013

Our very Dear
Father Vincent
Was a most wonderful priest
He was Mother Jozefa's
brother
And would usually come
At least twice a year
To Maryfield

He was
A True Blessing to us
Because
For many many years
He was very Faithful
In coming in June
To celebrate
The Sacred Heart Triduum
That we held

For the Big Feast of the
Sacred Heart
That is special to us
And ever so special to me
For the Sacred Heart
Is the Love of My Life

Father Vincent
Made these three days
beautiful
For he was always prepared
And his sermons
At the morning Mass
Flowed into those
At the evening Mass

We would have
Adoration of the Blessed
Sacrament
For a number of hours
On these special days
And at Benediction Time
Father would also include
Another little inspiring talk
for us
I believe
He had a special Joy
In coming to celebrate this
Triduum
For the Sacred Heart

During his spare time

He loved
To get out on the grounds
And mow the grass
He used to wear
And odd little hat
If I remember correctly
I believe it had
A little umbrella attached to it

Sometimes
He would come
For the
Feast of the Presentation of
Our Lady
In November
And more often
He would come
And celebrate
Our Christmas Masses
And give us the wonderful privilege
Of hearing 3 Masses
On Christmas Day

Father Vincent
Loved coming to Maryfield
And we loved
Having him
I pray that he is now enjoying
The delights and happiness
Of God's Heavenly Abode

⁓═⧫═⁓

Different Gifts
August 13, 2010

Father Vincent
Always liked to bring us
Some
I shall say
Different Gifts
Whenever he came for
Christmas
He had something
For each Sister

It might be
A toothbrush
Or
A funny hat
Or
Who knows what!

They were
Little gifts
But as each sister
Opened hers
They gave us
A Good Laugh

And you know

I think
That's really
What he was trying to do
Because
A good Laugh
Is very good
For the heart

Thank You Father Vincent!

○━━◆━━○

Father John Kowalewski
December 17, 2012

Father John Kowalewski
Is Mother Jozefa's brother
And he comes
Once a year
During Holy Week

He usually arrives
On Wednesday afternoon
After a long drive
From Childs, Maryland
Mother
Has spent some time
Helping and making sure
That his favorite meal is ready
And that

There is plenty of it
For our dear Father John
Is a big man
Tall
And with
A commanding figure
His Sister Chris
Who is so very dear
To his heart
Is the only one
Who can get away
With calling him
Santa Claus

After dinner
And visiting with Mother
He then gets some rest
Because
He will have to prepare
To celebrate
This most Holy
And Solemn Time
Of the year
Holy Thursday
Good Friday
Holy Saturday
And
The Great Feast of Easter
He really helps to make these days
Ever so beautiful and special

Sometimes
He adds
A unique touch
To the Mass
By giving us
The Last Blessing
In one of the African languages

Every year
Father John
Goes to South Africa
To help out
And to allow
The priests there a chance
To go on vacation
He just loves it
And the kids he teaches
Capture
A special place in his heart
He usually leaves in December
And doesn't return to the States
Until it is time
For our
Holy Week Services

At Mass
On Easter morn
Father gives us
Another beautiful sermon

Then we all go
To the Parlor
Where he meets us
Gives us
A special blessing
Then departs
Until next year

What a Wonderful Blessing
Father John
Has been to us!

May God Bless him
Forever!

Chris - The Special Child
May 31, 2010

Chris
Was Mother Jozefa's sister
Who she loved
So dearly

She was a Down Syndrome child
And Mother often spoke of
What A Great Blessing
She was
To their family

There was
No rejection of her
Just overwhelming love

They told her
She was a Princess
And she just beamed
In the thought

She was truly
Their Princess

Father John Comny
February 15, 2013

Father Comny
Was Mother Mary Jozefa
Kowalewski
Spiritual Director
For many years
While she was at
The Visitation Community
In Wilmington, Delaware
And then
When she came to our
Community
Here in Snellville, Georgia

We have been very blessed

By Father Comny's visits
Over the years
And he has become
Very dear
To our Community

We really enjoy
And find very helpful
The wonderful conferences
That he give us
He is always open
To questions
And I can hear him now
Saying
Are there any questions
I think he liked it
When it was
He seemed to really enjoy
Teaching
And especially
On Holy Father - St. Francis
de Sales
And his writings
He belonged to
The Oblates of St. Francis de
Sales
And he was a true son
Of Holy Father

Our Dear Father Comny
Departed this earth
Some years ago

I pray
That when he reached
Eternity
Our Dear Holy Father
St. Francis de Sales
Was there to greet him
And show him about
The Heavenly Kingdom

Remembering
February 16, 2013

Father Comny
Was usually with us
For Palm Sunday
And
A few days of talks
For our Holy Week Retreat

I will always remember
One bright
Palm Sunday day
After he had put on
The beautiful red vestment
His face
Took on
A very sweet countenance
And seemed to glow
With a pure white
Heavenly light

Father Tom Carroll

Father Tom Carroll
Is the Pastor
At Saint Oliver Catholic
Church
In Snellville, Georgia
On Tuesdays
He comes to say Mass for us
At the Visitation Monastery
Sometimes
Father Mike Flanagan comes
And sometimes
Father Cliff Hasler

St. Oliver's Parish
Is growing so much
That they have decided on
Another new addition
Because of this
For several months
Only Father Carroll has
been coming
To say our 8 am Mass
So that
He is able to attend
The weekly 9 am meeting
Concerning the new
building

On Monday
Father gave us a call
And I was later given a note
Since I work in the Sacristy
To change the vestment
And the Tabernacle veil
From green to white
Because tomorrow
Instead of just the Ordinary
Weekday Mass
We will be celebrating
The Feast Day of Our Lady
of LaSallette
This is the Feast Day of
Father's Order
He and Father Flanagan and
Father Cliff
And he wanted
To share it with us
Specially
He and Father Flanagan and
Father Cliff
Are LaSallette Priests

When Father Carroll came
on Tuesday
He brought a picture
Of Notre Dame Cathedral
In France
It showed the Swiss Alps
Rising high above it
It's the section of the
mountains
Where the Apparition
occurred

He also brought leaflets
For each Sister
With some of the details of
the story
And a beautiful book
With beautiful color
pictures
It tells the story of LaSallette
And how their Order was
Founded
Father also gave us
A lovely gift plate
That he had blessed
With Our Lady of LaSallette
on it
At Mass
He gave us
A beautiful homily too
On this Apparition

We were very grateful to
Father
And it really
Made the day so very special
But even more special
And most touching to the
heart
Was all the love

49

That filled his voice
As he spoke of Our Lady of
LaSallette
And his Order

Happy Feast Day
Father Carroll - Father
Flanagan - Father Cliff

c=⟩⟨=ɔ

Father Carroll's Book

Father Carroll
Is a great photographer
And he surprised us recently
By giving us
A lovely book
Filled with many of his
pictures
That had been taken
On vacations

There are beautiful
Scripture Quotes
To go with many of the
pictures
And in the beginning of the
book
He expressed Thanks
To those
Who helped him with these
quotes
And to Mrs. Dunn
Who suggested
That he should
Put his pictures on display
He did
And eventually decided
To publish a book

I thought it was really nice
That he dedicated it
To Father Flanagan and
Father Cliff

As I looked through the
pages
I saw a glorious sunrise
Majestic mountains -
Gushing waterfalls
Still Lakes - Mighty waters
Beautiful flower gardens
And a unique sand garden

I am so glad Father decided
To share his pictures
By publishing this book -
Images of Creation
For it soothes the soul
And gives your heart -
A Peaceful Joy

Part Two

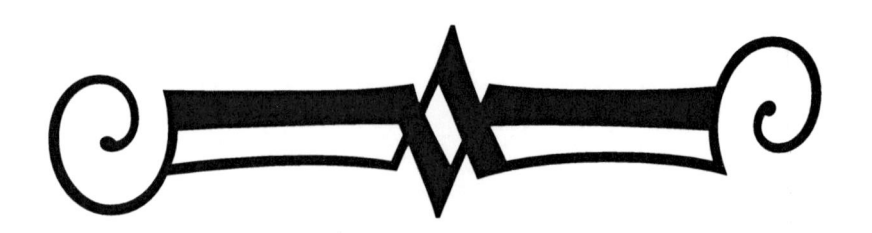

A Unique Description

This is a description
of our Chapel at Maryfield
using the Haiku poetry form

First Line ~ 5 syllables
Second Line ~ 7 Syllables
Third Line ~ 5 syllables

As it was in September 1998

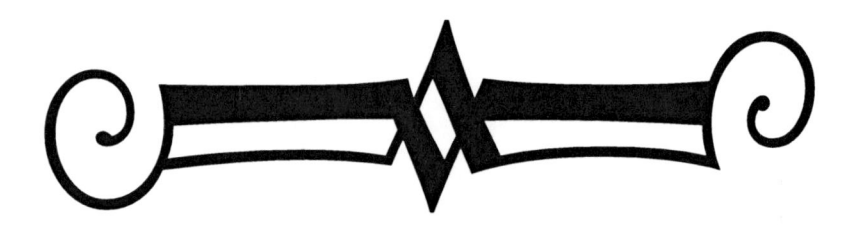

Two steps - wrought iron gate
Sacred Heart in vestibule
Welcomes the people

A golden dwelling
Surrounded by a white veil
The Most Precious Gift

Lovely shaped vases
Yellow ones, white, a pink one
Beautiful for God

Standing tall and grand
Six slender gold-topped candles
Behind - gold dwelling

In front of gold doors
Round golden candle-holders
Burn brightly in praise

Proclaimed from lecterns
Sacred Words that touch the soul
Listen and be wise

Left and near middle
Suspended covered table
Sacred vessels rest

Awe and Majesty
Shrouded Hidden Mystery
Lay on the altar

High above altar
Vertical Horizontal
Jesus was fastened

Many little greens
Overhanging brown baskets
Marble stands beneath

Wrapped in deep red glass
Near window hanging aloft
The Eternal Light

Silent and gentle
Holding babe over her heart
King and Queen of worlds

Quiet carpenter
Sweet Joseph of Nazareth
Special Protector

One stained glass window
A Heart that has so loved men
Saint of France - Paray

Another window
Pen writing on the pages
Saint Francis de Sales

Looking up I saw
Fortiter Fideliter
Bright rays shining thru

Little hideaway
Two chairs, vase on pedestal
Lady of the chair

Beneath the glass book
A heart surrounded by thorns
Order's - Court of Arms

Upon angel wings
As you enter thru the doors
A cleansing of soul

The Breath of My Life

In a special place
The Sacred Heart's arms outstretched
Overflowing Love

Below holy feet
Cranberry vase - silk flowers
A tucked-away chair

Shining from above
Casting down a mellow glow
A ceiling fixture

Silent flickering
Sitting in four red holders
Mounted on the wall

In a place close by
Names consecrated to Him
Hanging under a glass

Golden doors opened
In Presence of King of Kings
Kneel and Adore Him

Day of Mary's birth
Outside at new Lourdes Grotto
All said Rosary

Happy Birthday - Dear Mother

On an August day
As I admired the grotto
Tiny wings flew by

In special alcove
With a wall of light blue glass
Sweet Heart of Mary

Above the entrance
Imbedded in tones of blue
Lily - Pure and white

Huge needlepoint work
Jesus raises Lazarus
Mary M. Healy

Reliquary case
Sits under this huge glass frame
Filled with many Saints

On top of this case
Stands clear glass candle-holders
With two white candles

A Precious Book lies
On a special stand between
Holy Word of God

Precious silver cross
Holds relics of our Martyrs
Sent from Madrid, Spain

In a snug corner
Lady Admirabilis
Peaceful and serene

Face smiling slightly
Falls upon you at entrance
Saint Jane de Chantel

Keeping careful watch
Over all of his daughters
Saint Francis de Sales

Place - somewhat obscure
Saint Claude La Colombiere
Directed her soul

Beautiful statue
Of Saint Margaret Mary
Standing gracefully

Held within her hands
The Heart that has so loved men
A thin wooden plaque

Flowers - light purple
A little red votive light
Showing her honor

On floor - near one door
Plant - large green leaves - peace lilies
A big purple bow

Middle of Chapel
Above wood chairs and kneelers
Rays fall from skylight

From a small table
Sounds that lift you to Heaven
When zither is played

Organ melody
Raises voices up to God
In praise and honor

In new area
Special Monastic choir seats
Gift - sent from Ireland

Praises sung through day
From seats - carved
magnificent
The Divine Office

Sweet Holy Spirit
Thank you for inspiration
For this little book

After the Office
Lift seat - A hide-away shelf
Place for Office Books

On stand between choirs
Beautiful hand-made cover
On Office Bible

Small picture on wall
Lady clothed in black and gold
With a little child

Above area
Mary and Elizabeth
The Visitation

High the eagle soars
So much higher is the sky
Highest - Creator

Part Three

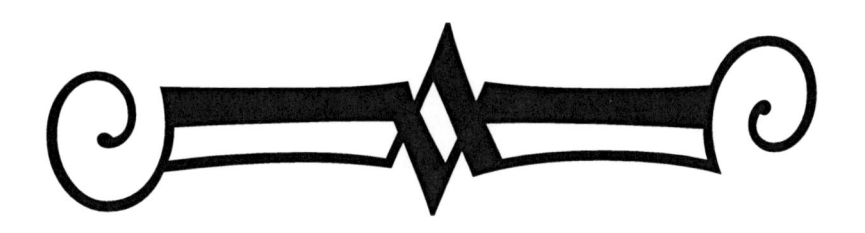

**Archbishop
Wilton D. Gregory
and
Some of his Priests**

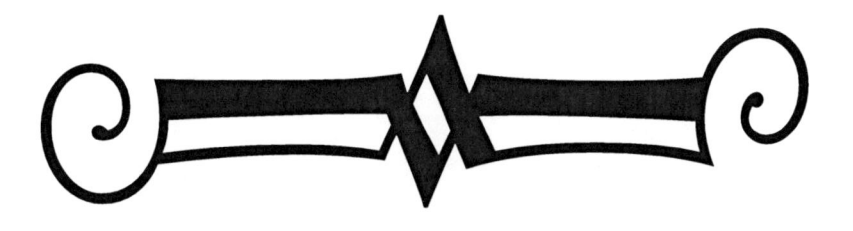

Archbishop Wilton Gregory
August 12, 2010

Our dear Archbishop
Wilton Gregory
Said Mass for us today
On this feast day
Of our Holy Mother
St. Jane de Chantal
August 12, 2010

His wonderful sermon
Showed a deep concern
For Family Life
He spoke of how
We thought
That Family Life
Would always be
A Reality
But now
Because society is changing
We have
A real breakdown
In Family Life
He then asked us to pray
For Vocations
Both Priests and Sisters
And to especially pray
For husbands and wives

New couples
And those preparing for marriage
That they will have
A Strong Family Life

He spoke on
Our Holy Mother
St. Jane de Chantal
And our being Founded
As a Religious Order
For 400 years
We have been celebrating it
All year

It began on January 24, 2010
The Feast of St. Francis de Sales
Our Holy Father
He was a Bishop
In Annecy, France
And together with Holy Mother
They founded our
Order of the Visitation of Holy Mary
On June 6, 1610
The official end of the Celebration
Will be
December 13, 2010

When Mass was over
The Archbishop
Had a short visit
With us in the parlor
Which we all enjoyed

Archbishop Gregory's Beautiful Voice
August 12, 2010

Archbishop Gregory
Has a most beautiful
Singing voice
As he joined us
In the hymns
And especially
When he sang
The Preface today
In such beautiful tones
You felt lifted up
Almost to Heaven

Another significant fact
He doesn't speed thru the hymns
And he doesn't
Rush thru the Mass
But shows
Proper Reverence
For this Sacred Celebration

And a great love
For what he is doing
Comes thru

We were grateful
That he could come
For we know
That he has
A very busy schedule

His beautiful voice
Brought back a memory
Of when I was a child
How!
I loved to sit
On my Father's lap
And listen
To the beautiful hymns
He would sing to me
I especially loved to hear him
Sing the song
Holy! Holy! Holy!
To me

My dear Father
Departed this world
In April - 1999
But for a long time
Whenever I heard the song
Holy! Holy! Holy!
I could hear

My Father's voice!

May God continue to bless
Archbishop Gregory
With that beautiful voice
So that he can always
Lift the hearts of those
around him
To the things of Eternity
To the things that really
matter

The Unforgettable Meeting
August 12, 2010

The Archbishop
Was a little pressed for time
To reach his next
engagement
But we could not let him
leave
Before meeting
The Two
Newest members
Of our community
Peter and Paul
Our Great Pyrenees
Peter smiled
And wagged his tail

But Paul
Decided to jump up
And greet him
Face to Face

I believe
Our dear Archbishop
Will agree
That it was a most
Unforgettable Meeting!

Three Things
December 11, 2010

Today - December 11, 2010
I heard
That the Archbishop's Father
Had passed away
To him I extend
Deep condolences and my
prayers

I did not know
Nor had I ever met
Mr. Wilton Gregory, Sr.
But there are
Three Things
I do know about him

He is

The Father of a son
Who is now
The Archbishop of Atlanta,
Georgia
And who is much loved
By the people
He Shepherds

He has given us
A son
Who has been of great
service
To the Church
Not only as Archbishop
But also
In the many other capacities
That he has served
And is still serving

Then
Very touchingly to the heart
Mr. Wilton, Sr.
Gave his son
The wonderful privilege
Of baptizing him
Into the Catholic Faith
What a Special Joy
For the both of them
What a Special Joy
For the Father and the Son

May God grant

Mr. Wilton Gregory, Sr.
The Peace of Paradise
And
May God grant
Archbishop Wilton Gregory
A Peaceful Heart!

Father Joseph Mendes
Our Beloved Chaplain
September 5, 2010

Today is Sunday
September 5, 2010
And it is
The Last Day
That Father Joseph Mendes
Will be our Chaplain
He has served us
So very well
For 13 years
And now
He must say
Good bye
And now
I must say
Something about
Our Beloved Chaplain

Father
Is deeply spiritual

Rooted in
A very deep
Love of God
He never ceases
Studying and Meditating
On the Word of God
And His marvelous wonders
How often
He speaks
Of being in awe
Of the Person of Jesus
Christ
The more
He contemplates Him
The more he finds
To contemplate
The more and deeper
His love grows
For Jesus
Our Divine Lord
And Savior
Therefore
As a Blessed Result
Everyday
Father's homily
Is like
A mini Spiritual Conference
And on Sundays
It is a more expanded one
In them
He shows us
The Love of God

And just how much
God loves and cares for us

He also gives us
Insight
So that we can see
The need
To repent of our sins
The need
To correct our faults and failings
The need
To practice virtues
Patience - gentleness - kindness
To stop the gossip - rash judgments
And so forth
To love and bear with our neighbor
And to remember
That from time to time
We will cause our neighbor
To try
To bear with us

Most Importantly
And to sum up everything
Father tells us
To keep God
First!
In our lives

Even amid
Trials and difficulties

Then he reminds us
That whatever gifts we have
We should use them
To Glorify God!

Father has
A very special love
For Our Lady
And loves to celebrate
Her special days and feasts

On Saturdays
He uses
A special Sacramentary for Mass
Blue of course
That is arranged
With Masses
Just to honor her
He even tries to get me
To give him
A big feast day
Very special vestment
For these regular Saturdays
I say
Father
If I give you
A big feast day vestment
Every Saturday

Then what will I give you
When the Big Feast day comes
So he tries to content himself
With Our Lady's
Saturday Vestment

Father too
Has a great love
For St. Francis de Sales
And rightly so
Because
He is a
Missionary of St. Francis de Sales
And this Religious Order
Claims him
For their patron

Therefore
He is akin to us
And shares
Some of our spirituality
Which helps him
To understand us better
And our Way of Life

Whenever he can
Father will quote
Some saying
Of St. Francis de Sales

In his homily
Or when
He is talking to you
As he does
You will see
His face light up with love
He is surely
A True Son
Of St. Francis de Sales

On the First Friday
Of each month
We also have
An Evening Mass at 7:30 p.m.
In honor of the Sacred Heart
And Father
Has been so wonderful
In having
This second Mass of the day for us
Our Order was chosen
For this
Special Devotion to the Sacred Heart
When Our Lord appeared
To St. Margaret Mary
A Visitation Nun in France
And revealed to her
In three Great Revelations
His desire

For this devotion

Father
Prepares these sermons
Especially
For the Sacred Heart
Who is
The Love of My Life
They are very enriching
And our dear Chaplain
Even comes
About an hour early
To hear Confessions
Of those attending Mass
If they would like to go
Truly
A special blessing
For the congregation

Deacon Michael Mobley
Comes and assists him
And has been
So very faithful
For many years
That we claim him
As our Deacon
He and Father
Really make
Our First Friday
Celebrations
Very Beautiful
Another

Beautiful Something
That Father does
Is during
May and June
And I think
It is somewhat
Unique

On Mother's Day
And
On Father's Day
Father Mendes will ask
All the Mothers
And all the Fathers
On their day
To come forward
Right after Mass
And gather around him
By the Sanctuary
He then gives them
A most uplifting
Little talk
And using
The Book of Blessings
And holy water
He bestows upon them
A very Special Blessing
That I believe
Really touches their hearts

I could go on
But this will suffice

To say something
About Our Beloved
Chaplain

May God Bless him Forever
And someday
Bestow upon him
Eternal Peace and Rest
In the Golden Land of
Paradise

P.S.
Most of the time
Father calls me
Sister
But sometimes
He calls me
Sister Sacred Heart
And other times
Just
Sacred Heart
I am sure going to miss you
Fr. Mendes

⚜

Father Juan
August 5, 2010

Father Juan
Is a
Young Priest

That has been coming
To say Mass for us
On Wednesdays and
Thursdays
For several months

He gives us
Beautiful homilies
Filled with insight
That can really help
Your daily life
That can really help you
On the Way to Salvation

He has
A deep love
And reverence for Mass
And even
When he is pressed for time
He does not
Rush the Mass

May God Forever
Keep him close to Him
And someday
Bless him
With the Riches of Paradise

P.S.
Whenever he can
Father likes to spend
Some quiet time

In Recollection
To prepare himself For Mass
Then
He will finish
Getting ready for Mass

One morning
When I happened
To come into the Sacristy
While he was vesting
It was very touching
To see how reverently
He kissed his stole

⁘━━⋎━━⁘

The Senior Discount
August 5, 2010

When I went
To get flowers yesterday
I received
A Senior Discount
I wondered
If I am now beginning
To Look My Age!

Most of my life
People think
I am a lot younger
So it's a revelation to me
If it's otherwise

This morning
When
Father Juan came for Mass
He forgot to tuck away his homily
In the Lectionary
As he usually does
Therefore
I asked him about it
Before I took the Books out
Into the Chapel
He said
Oh!
That's how it is
When you are getting old!

I then told him
When I was his age - 29
I was thinking along those lines
I went on to tell him
When I was around 15 or so
In my teens
I thought 30 something
Was definitely old
When I reached 25
I was not looking happily
To making that 30 years old
The Big Three 0!
Well!
I survived it!

And next I thought
Surely!
I will be resting
On My Precious Sacred Heart
Before I was 50!
Then on that Birthday
I woke up
And found myself
Half-a-Century!
Apparently
The Sacred Heart
Had other plans for me
Now!
I told him
I am 62
And will soon have to admit
I am Old!
Especially
Since I was given
That Senior Discount
For flowers yesterday
Father Juan
Looked somewhat stunned
And asked me to repeat
I told him again
That I was 62
He simply
Could not believe it!
He thought I was about 40 or 41
Thanks Father Juan!

My Youth Is Restored!

The Conversation
February 20, 2013

One day
Father Juan spoke of
How much the people
Really loved the Archbishop
He said
Whenever they know he is coming
They are ready to do all they can
To make him welcome
Father Juan also said
That he was like
A father to him
Very caring
And I could see
He was truly
Sincere

Father John DeVore
April 11, 2011

As I worked on
Preparations for Holy Week
I thought about
Father Devore today

He used to come sometime
And con-celebrate Mass
On Easter Day
It was always
A Joy
To have him

I remember
Sometimes
When I would go
To answer the door
There he would be standing
With a big smile
Holding
Some special goodies
For us
He seemed to have
A real joy
In bringing them
And we
Truly enjoyed them

Recently - January, 2011
Father celebrated
His Silver Jubilee
And I heard
It was
A Wonderful Event
Last year

Father Devore could not come
To con-celebrate
For he is not
As well as he used to be
But Oh!
How glad I was
To hear
That he will be coming
To con-celebrate our Mass
This Easter Day!

May God bless
Father Devore
And some day
Bring him to
That Grand Easter
Celebration
In the Golden Land
Of His Heavenly Kingdom

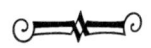

⚜

Father James Henault
July 4, 2011
Father Jim
Is the pastor
Of St. Oliver Pluckett's
Catholic Church
In Snellville, Georgia
And it is the parish
Where our Monastery is located

The parish
Has really grown
Over the years
And I believe
They now have
Around 2500 families
registered

When the Sisters
Moved into this Monastery
In 1974
The Chapel was used
As the parish church
What a difference
Between
Now and Then!

As I look thru
The Church Bulletin
I have noticed
Some of the additions
And improvements
That Father Jim has made
That help to make things
Beautiful
For worship of the Lord
And as smooth running
As possible
I believe the parishioners
Are quite thankful

For what he has done

Sometimes
He comes to say Mass for us
On Tuesdays
Which is our Chaplain's
Day Off
Most of the time
He lets his Assistant come
Father Neil Jones
However
When Father Jim does come
He gives us
A most insightful sermon
He then does
The Intercessions
And when he finishes them
He has us join him
In a Hail Mary
For these intentions
I think
He must have
A very special place
For Our Lady
In his heart
And I am sure
This must be ever so
pleasing
To her
May
Our Dear Lady of LaSallette
In whose Order

Father Jim belongs
Always keep him
Close to her heart
And may
Our Dear Lord
The Good Shepherd
Always lead and guide him
And help him
To lead his flock
Along the way
To Salvation

⁌—⚜—⁍

July 8, 2011

Father Jim
Has a special friend
Who likes
To go about with him
I understand
That sometimes
He even accompanies Father
Jim
On his trips
I am sure
This is a real delight
To him
This special friend
Of Father Jim
Is known
As Yoda

His forever faithful
Little Chihuahua

―――

Father Neil Jones
July 4, 2011

Father Neil
Resides at
St. Oliver Pluckett's
Catholic Church
In Snellville, Georgia
He is Father Jim Henault's
Assistant Pastor

Most Tuesdays
He comes
To say Mass for us
Because our regular
Chaplain
Is off that day

He usually arrives
A little early
And is vested
And waiting near the door
To reach me the books
The Sacramentary
And The Lectionary
When I come
We exchange greetings

And a few other words
And then He tells me
I have just a few minutes
To light the candles
And set up the books
For Mass
I tell him
I have more time
Then he thinks
Because
We are on
Monastery Time
It doesn't matter
What his watch has
We live by
The sound of the bell
And it's not 8:30 a.m.
Until
The Monastery Bell says so

One time
When he happened
To see Mother outside
When he drove up
He didn't come right in
Because
He spent a few minutes
Talking to her
When he did come in
I believe
I remarked
About his being later

He told me
He was on
Monastery Time!

I was somewhat surprised
To learn
That Father Neil
Loves to cook
And has become
Very good at it
From what I understand
He loves to go
To Rome, Italy
On vacation
And I remember
One year
He told me
He would be attending
A cooking school
For around a week
I guess
Learning different
Gourmet Specialties

From time to time
I see
In St. Oliver's Church
Bulletin
That there will be
An International Day
And foods from different
lands

Will be served
Father Neil's specialty
Is of course included
And last summer
Or the summer before
He told me
He would be cooking up
Something good
For a lot of young people
Who worked on
A Special Project
In their Parish
I am sure
They enjoyed it

One time
When we had
A special celebration
And afterwards
We had
A little something
For the people
In the Parlor
Father Neil
Had time to stay
And our Community
Had a wonderful
Little visit with him
We really enjoyed it
And it brought
A special happiness
To our day

May God forever
Bless and keep
Our Dear Father Neil
And someday
Bring him home
To Paradise

P.S.
Father Neil
Served our Country
For six years
As a Navy Chaplain
And the war
Desert Storm
Was a part of those six years

I want to say
Thank you Father
We are so very grateful

○━━◆━━○

Father Neil's Sermons
July 3, 2011

Father Neil
Always gives us
A very good sermon
They are short and quick
But they are
Powerful and to the point

They make you think
About some aspect of your life
And he may cause you
To ask yourself
What are you doing about it

If we heed
What he says
We will grow
In our spiritual life
And come
Ever closer to God

○━━◆━━○

A Beautiful Moment
July 3, 2011

Father Neil's Mass
Is not quite as long
As our other
Weekday Masses
Because
Sometimes
He has to hurry back
To St. Oliver's
To say the 9 am Mass
However
I must say
His 8:30 Mass for us
Does not seem

To be rushed

When I happened
To look up from my prayer
After Communion
One morning
His head was bowed
In a few moments of silent prayer
At the Altar

What a beautiful moment
To behold

How uplifting
To the heart

○═╋═○

Father Michael Hogan
September 20, 2011

Not too very long ago
I happened
To run into Father Hogan
While I was out
He used to be our Chaplain
But is now retired

I remember
How he loved
To wear

Our Lady's Vestments
On her special feast days
And they really did
Look nice on him

I remember too
The Joy
That he gave us
At Christmas
Each Sister
Would receive
A special little gift
So beautifully wrapped

I especially remember too
Father's deep concern for us
He was a good Chaplain
And we loved him

He looked well
When I saw him
May God continue
To bless him
In his retirement years
And someday
Bring him
Safely home to Heaven

Father John Fallon
September 21, 2011

Father Fallon
Has been our Confessor
For many years

We can always
Depend on him
To come
Once a week

Sometimes
He may not be able
To come
On the usual day
But he tries to call
And come
Another day that week

He also comes
For Benediction
On Sunday afternoons
Despite
His busy schedule
And his prison ministry

We are
Ever so grateful to him
And really appreciate
His Faithfulness

May God
Always lead and guide him
And someday
Bring him into
The Light of His Glory

The Prisoner's Priest
September 21, 2011

Father Fallon
Has had
A prison ministry
For many years

It really is
A special call
And he takes his duty
Very serious

He has
A deep concern
For all those
That he ministers to
And he tries
To help them
In any way
That he can

Whenever
He goes back to Ireland
On vacation
They really miss him

I remember
A Christmas Season
Years ago
When Father asked
To borrow
One of our Altar cloths
He wanted everything
To look nice
For those attending Mass
During this
Special Time

We thought
It was
A very beautiful thing
For him to do
To try to uplift those
He ministered to

I know these prisoners
Are ever so grateful
To Father Fallon
For his dedication to them
May God reward him -
Abundantly
For all he does

Father Sunny Punnakuziyil
September 23, 2011

Father Sunny Punnakuziyil
Became
Our new Chaplain
Last September - 2010

Our Dear Chaplain
Father Joseph Mendes
Was leaving us
After 13 years
I still miss him
But we have come to love
Father Sunny very much too

He is from India also
Like Father Mendes
But shortly after Ordination
He was sent
To the Philippines
And he was there
For around 15 years
Soon
After he arrived
God granted him
A very special favor
He got a chance to see
And I believe concelebrate

Mass with
Our Beloved
Pope John Paul II
Who is now
Blessed Pope John Paul II
It is an event
That he cherishes
And I am sure
Will never forget

Then
God stepped in
With a new plan
For his life
He sent him
To us!
And
How happy we are
To have him
For our Chaplain

Like Father Mendes
He too
Gives us very good sermons
That help us deepen
Our Spiritual Life

When there is
Some special intention
For Mass
Father doesn't fail
To mention

The person's name
Or the intention
Several times
During the Mass
It is really touching
To those attending
Who may have lost
A loved one

Father Sunny
Helped out at St. Matthews
In Winder
For a time
And now
That he is no longer there
Sometimes
A few of the Parishioners
Will attend Mass here
Because
They really miss him

One gentleman told me
That Father Sunny
Had the right name
Because
He had a sunny disposition
And was just
Filled with love

I definitely agree
With that gentleman

May God Forever Bless
Our Dear Father Sunny
And someday bring him
Into that light
That is brighter
Than the sun

Father Sunny and the Clock
September 22, 2011

A while back
Father Sunny told
A little story
During his sermon
That he had heard or read
And it was really
Helpful to me

He said
There was a clock
Who started noticing
How it ticked
So he decided
To count all the ticks
That he made
In an hour
Than
In a day
And on and on

Until he came
To the total
For the year
I don't remember
How many it was
For a year
But it was
So Overwhelming
For the clock
That he had
To seek a doctor
To try to keep
From having
A Nervous Breakdown!

The doctor
Listened to the clock
As he poured forth
All his anxiety
About those thousands
And thousands
Of Ticks!
He would have to make
A year
When he finished
The doctor told him
To concentrate
On making
Just one tick
At a time

He was not to worry

About all those thousands
For a year
But!
To just take
One at a time

This consoled the clock
And he thereafter went
happily
Ticking along

Father told us this story
A short time before Easter
As Sacristan
I always have to check ahead
To see what feast days
Are coming up
So that
I can prepare for them

As I was looking
Thru the Sacristy Ordo
I noticed
That after
The Annunciation
On March 25th
I would soon have to start
Preparing for Holy Week
The busiest week
In the Sacristy
And which calls for
Two or Three weeks
preparation ahead

After this
I went on
Looking thru the Ordo
And I saw
There was just
Feast after Feast
For months
Also including
The Sacred Heart Triduum
A time
When we have
Two Masses a day

In honor of the
Feast of the Sacred Heart
Besides this
We were having a Sister
Making her First Profession
She would be taking
Temporary Vows for 3 years
And we were also having
A Sister
Taking her Final Vows
And receiving her black veil
This would be August 7, 2011
After this
It would be the feast
Of Our Holy Mother
St. Jane de Chantal

August 12th
And then
The Feast of the Assumption
Of Our Lady
On August 15th

From March to August
Except for around 2 weeks
in July
I would hardly
Have time
To catch my breath

Oh My! My!
I was overwhelmed!
Then I remembered
The clock!
And I thought
The only way
I can get thru this
Is like the clock
I resolved
That I would only look at
One!
Feast day at a time

Thanks be to God!
I made it thru!
Though I was
Exhausted!

Thank you Father Sunny!

For your sermon on the clock!

Part Four

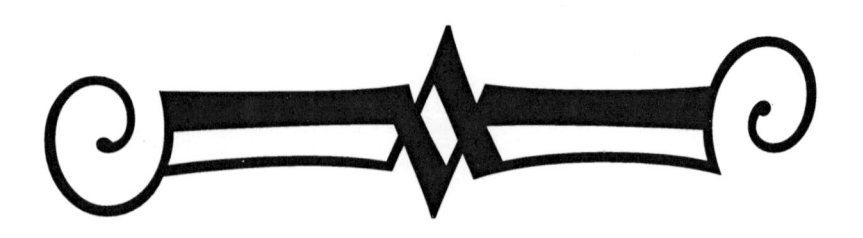

Golden Memories
of
My Dear Parents
and
My Dear Aunt Martha

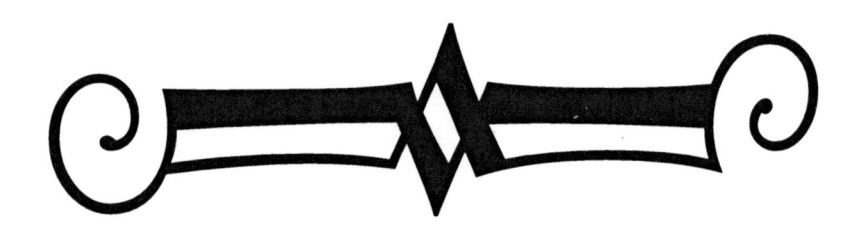

O Daddy Dear
June 17, 2007

O Daddy Dear
How I love you!

O Daddy Dear
How I miss you!

Today
Is Father's Day
And my mind is filled
With thoughts of you

You've been gone 8 years
And I can hardly believe it
But it is true
For you departed this earth
On Friday - April 23, 1999

How Good!
You were to me!
There is nothing
Under the sun
That you wouldn't have
done for me
If it was within your power
For I was - Daddy's girl
From the time
I was a babe

Mother said
You would get my things
together
And off we would go
On the bus
For a visit to your sister
Apparently
When I was a babe
They didn't have a car
But that didn't stop Daddy
For he loved
To take me about
And it never stopped
All during my school days

All my life
I could depend on him
And My Dear Mother
No matter
What place in the world
I found myself in
They were as close
As the telephone
There would always be
someone
At the unchanging number
Of 318-442-2528
And that steadfast address
Of 620 Hunter Street
In Pineville, Louisiana
Zip - 71360

Now
You both are gone
And what
A Distinct Absence
In my life

But I know
O Daddy Dear
That you both
Are watching over me
And waiting for the day
When I will depart this earth
And then
O Daddy Daddy Dear
You can once again
Take me about
In a Land
Whose beauty
I have never known

O Daddy Dear
How I love You!

O Daddy Dear
How I Miss You!

Sweet Susie
February 22, 2011

My Dear Cousin
Susie Holmes
Was so very sweet

She was always smiling
And seemed to be
Bubbling Joy
Almost always

I remember
When I was young
And still in grade school
My Father
Took me along
On a visit to see her -
Not too long
After she was married
She had made
Some home-made yeast rolls
In a number of clever designs
Some were made
Like dinner rolls
And I remember
In particular
That some were made
In the shape
Of braids of hair

Oh! how good they were!
Oh! how I loved them!

My Dear Cousin
Sweet Susie
Has now departed this earth
May she
Spend her Eternity
Bubbling over
In the Joys of Heaven

Rev. Leroy Holmes

I thought about
My Sweet Susie's
Dear husband Leroy
He was a minister
Helping to lead people
Closer to God

He had a quiet
And gentle disposition
And I don't believe
That I ever heard him
Raise his voice

He departed this earth
Some years before her
I pray
That Our Lord was there
To welcome him
Into the peace and joy
Of Heaven

Sweet Susie's Children
November 23, 2009

I thought about
My cousin Susie's
Children today
Her daughter Lanette
And her son
Leroy Holmes, Jr.
I have not seen them
In so many years
I wondered
How they were

Lanette
Married a minister
And the last I heard
They had around 4 children
And were living in Texas I believe
Leroy, Jr.
As he was called
Went to California
Long ago
And there
He too became
A minister
Like his father

I hope

Life has treated them well
And I pray
That if our paths
Never cross again
Upon this earth
May God
Someday let them cross
In Paradise

God-Willing
August 22, 2010

In talking
To my Father
If you made
Some request of him
Or
If he was making plans
To do something
Or perhaps
Planning to go on a trip
He would always say
God willing - I will do
Such and such a thing
God-willing - I will go
To such and such a place

It was just
His usual way of speaking
And I did not really reflect

on it
When I was growing up
But looking back now
I can see
Shining forth
The Beauty
Of the Presence of God
In his life

August 21, 2010

When Father Mendes
Came for Mass this morning
I noticed
That he had gotten
A very close hair-cut
He called it
His summer crop

It made me think
Of days long ago
When my son Bobby
Was a little boy
Every Saturday morning
He and Daddy
Would set out
For the barber shop
Neither one
Had much hair to cut
But off they went

Every Saturday morning

They just liked
Being together
And made
Quite a morning of it

They would go and visit
My Father's sister
Dear Aunt Blanche
Or perhaps elsewhere
And maybe have lunch
Or stop somewhere
For some goodies

Eventually
They would return
And
Look Forward
To the next
Saturday morning

Daddy's Gift
August 21, 2010

Thinking
On those Saturday morning haircuts
Of Bobby and Daddy
Brought to mind

Two Special Times
Of the year
Christmas and Easter

Sometimes
Daddy
Would pick Bobby up
During this seasonal time
And they would go
shopping
For Christmas or Easter
Clothes and shoes

I tell you
When Christmas or Easter came
How good
Bobby would look
In those 3- piece suits
That Daddy would buy for him

How grateful I was for this gift!

P.S.
Let me also say
How good Daddy looked
In his
Three-piece suits

Untitled 1
August 22, 2010

One day
When someone
Did a favor for me
I was about
To thank them
When I remembered
My Father's words
That I had heard him use sometimes
I appreciate your kindness
To the highest

So I thought
I would thank the person
In like manner

Since then
From time to time
When a favor
Is done for me
You may hear me
Use my Father's words
I appreciate
Your kindness
To the highest

Feast Day of St. Francis de Sales
January 24, 2011

Daddy
Loved to cook his breakfast
And every now and then
He cooked dinner
He really was
Quite a good cook
And at Christmas Time
He became
Quite a good baker
For he loved to make cakes
And they were
Really delicious
Especially
The yellow cake
With his thick and creamy
Homemade white frosting

He and my Grandmother
Mama Pearl
Would be in the kitchen
Baking away
Until we had
Oh so many
Cakes and Pies!

P.S.

It was also a time
That they liked
To go to
The Green Stamp store
And the Community Coffee store
For they saved stamps and coupons
All year
And at Christmas Time
Daddy and my Grandmother would go
And bring back
New cake and pie pans
And other nice
And useful things for the kitchen
It was
A real joy
For them each year

⚜

Daddy's Gravy
January 24, 2011
St. Francis de Sales Feast Day

We had a special dinner today
For the Feast of St. Francis de Sales

As I enjoyed the gravy
I thought of the gravy
My Father used to make

He browned his flour well
Added water
And cut up onions in it
Added meat and other seasonings
And cooked it a while
It was ever so good!

Mother always did the cooking
Except sometimes
But every now and then
When she wanted gravy
She would ask my Father
To fix it
She knew it would be Super Good!

⚜

Daddy's Saying
September 25, 2010

Today I thought about
One of Daddy's sayings
When you were going on and on

91

In a teasing way
He would say
You are full of stuff
As a Christmas turkey

Untitled 2
August 22, 2010

Many of us know
Something about
The Three Stages
In the Spiritual Life
The Purgative
The Illuminative
The Unitive

Within these stages
We struggle and strive
And try to reach
That height of perfection
That God has destined for us
From All Eternity

I do not believe
That my Father
Knew anything
About these three stages
Of the Spiritual Life
But in a simple way

He prayed to reach
The very Height of
Perfection
That God had destined for him

This was his prayer

He said:
I ask the Lord
To forgive me
For any little thing
That I have done wrong
During the day

And I tell Him
I don't want
Any other place
Just the one
That he has
Prepared for me
And no other

Precious Time
January 30, 2004

The sun was shining brightly
As I left the Alexandria
Airport
That November day

This Fall of 2003
Had been quite warm
And how I loved it!

I had been on a visit home
For two months
To help my dear Mother of 91
She is still living on her own
With my dear Aunt Martha
Who is 81 and retarded
But who has been
Such a wonderful help to her
In her time of need

My Mother
Has been amazed
At the beautiful deeds of charity
She has done for her
She often says
That she never thought
My Sweet Aunt Martha
Would be able to do
Some of them

I tell her
That I know
God is going to Bless her
With a Wonderful Place
In Heaven

It was a very busy time
While I was there
Because the house
Was in need of some major repairs
But I am so very grateful
To My God
For that Precious Time
That I was able
To spend with My Mother
For I know
I may never have
That opportunity again

As I walked
Toward the plane that day
I could see her clearly
She was wearing
A pretty blue and white dress
With a little cap
That was rolled up all around
She was waving
And she had a smile
On her face
That was brighter than the sun
I threw her a kiss
And she threw me one
I then boarded the plane

For my return trip to
Atlanta
But this picture of her
Will forever be
Etched
In my memory

October 24, 2006

I thought about
Mrs. Etta today
She was our neighbor
Who lived across the street
In front of us
When I was a babe

Though we moved
When I was around 6 years old
And later she moved
From time to time
Thru the years
She would come
To visit my Mother
And the family

What I particularly
Remembered today
Was her kindness
To My Dear Mother
While she was in
The Nursing Home
The last year of her life

Mrs. Etta
Knew that Mother
Loved sweets
So she would surprise her
From time to time
By bringing her
A few pieces of
Sweet Potato Pie

How Mother's face would
light up
With a big smile
And beaming eyes
Mother knew
Ms. Etta was a good cook
And she thoroughly enjoyed
every bite

I can never
Thank her enough
For those little special visits
That warmed Mother's heart
so
I pray that God
Will reward her abundantly
In this life
And may she one day dwell
In His Peaceful Land

October 29, 2006

I thought about
Mrs. Smith today
She was a long-time friend
Of my Mother
I believe her husband
Worked with my Father
At the Veteran's Hospital

She loved to bake cakes
And sometimes
She would bring us one
Or call for someone
To pick it up
How good they were!
How Mother loved them!

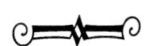

First Friday
November 3, 2006

I thought about
Mother's home-made
biscuits
She could really make them
And as many would say
They just melted in your
mouth

How my Father
Really loved them!

All Saints Day
November 1, 2006

I thought about
Mrs. Bernice
Mother's beautician
For many years

Mother went
Every Saturday
Much of the time
And would get her hair
Styled in what was called
A Finger Wave

She wore it
For many years
And it was
So becoming on her
I believe the only picture
My Father carried of her
In his wallet
Was one of long ago
Where she was wearing
A finger wave
Mrs. Bernice
Really knew how

To put in those waves
She had
What I would call
A Magic Touch

They stayed friends
Until the Lord called
Mrs. Bernice away
So many many years ago

November 1, 2006

I remember
How Mother
Loved to go to Church
She would start out
Going to Services at her Church
In the morning
Then attending Services at another Church
In the Afternoon
Then after that
Attending Night Services
At her Church or some other
Sometimes
There were even trips out of town
For Special Church Events

I remember hearing her say
That when she was growing up
In the Country
That the Minister said
The Church Bell didn't ring
Without her being there

All Saints Day
November 1, 2006

Today
I thought about
How Mother loved
To visit the country
To see family and friends

We would leave early
And go and spend the day
We enjoyed seeing
As many as we could
And I would have a jolly time
With my cousins

Of course
We all enjoyed
Those good country
Cakes and pies

Sometimes
Someone unexpected
Would stop in
Sometimes
It was someone
They had not seen in years
And sometimes
It would be
Someone you had never seen
But in talking
You find out
It is one of your distant
relatives
And oh! What rejoicing
Would go on!

Oh how!
I can hear
Mother's happy laughter
In those days
Long gone by

Mrs. Alma Mills
November 15, 2010

I thought about
Mrs. Alma Mills today
She was a nice lady
In our neighborhood

A few years ago
When I was home
Taking care of my Mother
I happened
To walk by her house
When my Dear Aunt
Martha and I
Were going to pay her
Church Dues
On the way back
We stopped by

I had not seen her
In many years
Her daughter Shirley
Answered the door
And showed us in
To my surprise
There was Mrs. Mills
At about 95 years old
Attending to something
In her oven

She didn't look
In any way
Near 95
And I was informed
That on Sundays
She walked
To Church
Amazing!

Aunt Martha and I
Did not stay long
But before we left
They took a few pictures
And not too long after
They dropped off
A few copies for us
When they were
On their way to Vote!
God has certainly blessed
Mrs. Alma Mills
May he continue to do so
And someday
May He grant her
And her daughter
The Gift of Paradise

Mrs. Jessie Marzett
February 15, 2009

Miss Jessie
As I called her
Was our neighbor
She lived
Just a few houses away
Her husband died
When I was very young
And she had to raise
Two small boys alone
She worked at the same hospital
Where my Aunt Blanche worked
My Father's sister

She always went to church
And even more so
In her later years
She sung in the choir
And traveled about with them
In town
And out of town

I really can't thank
Miss Jessie enough
For all her goodness and kindness
In helping Mother
When Daddy was ill
She would stay with him
Whenever Mother had to go out
To take care of business

After he died
When Mother wasn't well
She would come
To check on her
And Aunt Martha

I remembered
Daddy calling her Couz -

sometime
But I thought nothing of it
To my surprise
I just recently found out
That she is
Somehow thru the generations
A real true cousin of ours
I will forever be grateful to her
For all that she did
For my parents
And Aunt Martha

Miss Jessie died
In November, 2008
May God show her
His Gratitude
In Paradise
For all she has done

To have them all filled
To the brim!

They were old-fashioned looking
Glass canisters
With red knobs
On the top of the lids
And she kept them filled
With sugar, rice, flour
Grits and meal
I believe each one held
around 5 lbs.

I don't remember
Where she got them
But they were
A part of her kitchen
For many many years

Mother's Jars!
August 1, 2010

Mother's Jars!
Mother's Jars!
How she loved them!

It was such a delight
To her

Hats!
July 15, 2010

Thinking of the poem
Sunday Best
I remembered
How my Mother
Loved Hats!

She loved to dress

And she had a hat
To go with
Almost anything

They ranged
From inexpensive
To very expensive

When she dressed up
She really did look good
And her hat
Was that added touch!

The Special Angel
February 18, 2013

When my Mother
Was a resident
Of
The Oaks Care Center
In Pineville, LA
There was a lady
Who would keep
A special eye on her

If Mother needed
Some kind of help
Or something extra special
She would try
To see to it

Or let me know
If I
Could not reach Mother
On the phone
And became concerned
I would call this lady
And she would gladly
Check on her
Aunt Fannie
Would also do the same

This lady
Really did love Mother
So much so
That she called her
Mama

She would come
And visit her
And they would just
Laugh and talk
For quite a while
They truly enjoyed
Each other's company

And sometimes
This lady
Would bring her
A sweet treat
She loved that!

This lady

Has been in two or three
Other Nursing Home
Facilities
For a total
Of around 25 years
Sometimes
She has visitors
Who come and thank her
For all the care and help
That she gave
Their loved one
While she was near them

Though
My Dear Mother
Is no longer here
I still visit
This lady often
For she has become
So very dear to my heart
And I truly believe
That this dear lady
Ms. Betty Basco
Is
A Special Angel
Sent by God
To help our loved one
In these care centers

How grateful I am to Ms. Betty
For all her goodness and
kindness
To my Mother
Which I can never repay
And
How very grateful I am to
God
For this Special Angel

When she leaves this world
And is lifted up
Into those Heavenly realms
May God grant her
Wings of Gold
And shower her
With gifts and treasures
untold

Ms. Theresa
March 7, 2013

A friend of Ms. Betty
And Mother's too
Was Ms. Theresa
Her room was directly across
From Mother's room
She was a very nice lady
And had a rather
Soft sweet voice

One day

She really came
To Mother's aid
Even though
She was bedridden
Somehow she knew
Mother needed help
She immediately rang for someone
And Mother received
The immediate help
That she needed

I was so very grateful
To Ms. Theresa

I pray
That the day
She left this world
The Angels came
And greeted her
And then took her Home
To Paradise

Mother's Squirrel
August 7, 2013

Sometimes
When I talked on the phone
To Mother
She would tell me
About a little squirrel
That was brave enough to come
Right up to the screen door
Looking for
The slice or two of bread
That she would
Throw out to him
I believe sometime
I had to hold on
While she took care
Of this little friend

One day
When I was on a visit home
I happened to see a squirrel
Sitting on top of the mailbox
He looked to be
Waiting for something
Then I thought
This must be
Mother's squirrel!
So I went to the kitchen
But before I could return
I heard a loud scratching
Upon the screen door
I guess
I was just taking too long
To bring his snack!

December 27, 2005

Mother
Did not work in the yard
much
But I remember
How she loved flowers!

One particular year
We had some beautiful ones
That she had a special love
for
Planted on each side of the
walkway
I believe she called them
Rooster Cones
But I do not know their
proper name
These she planted
With her own hands
And their beauty
Was a joy and delight
To her heart

The Last Time
February 15, 2009

Shortly

Before Mother became
A Resident
At the Oaks Care Center
Terry McCall
Came home from California
For a visit
He grew up in our
neighborhood
A few houses away
He has become a minister
And is now
Rev. Terry McCall
Mother
Really wanted
To hear him preach
While he was in town

God granted her
This wish
For Terry's wife
Had the kindness
To pick her up
And take her to the Service

Terry's wife
Also took Mother's picture
On that special day
She was all dressed in white
And she looked beautiful
And still at 92
She retained
Her love of hats

103

So of course
She also wore
A most becoming white hat
To match her outfit

Again
She looked beautiful
As she stood
In front of home

I am so grateful
To Terry
And his dear wife
For fulfilling
Mother's wish
For it was
The Last Time
She attended Church
Before she left home

May God Bless them
Always
And someday
Grant them paradise

Mother's Silver
August 27, 2009

I happened
To walk down to the Parlor
This morning - August 27, 2009
As I looked about
I soon beheld
A Sweet Remembrance
My Dear Mother's
Precious Silverware Chest
From years of long ago
For I was just a child
When she bought it

She kept it on the Buffet
And when she had
Special Company
She would take it out
And use it

It has
A very beautiful pattern design
There are 2 roses
Toward the top of most pieces
And the overall design
Is somewhat ornate
She loved it!
And I loved it!

When I entered
Religious Life
And took

My Final Vows
She sent it to me
As a gift
A Most Wonderful Gift
Plus
A very good set
Of cooking pots - that I
loved too
That she had for years
But had never used
Except for 1 or 2
That she had taken out

My Final Profession
Was in June 1996
A little over 13 years ago
And I can't tell
How many times
Mother's silver has been used
But
It has truly been
A Blessing for us
For so many occasions
Like celebrations of Vows
being taken
Golden Jubilees - Silver
Jubilees
Archbishops visiting or
Priests
And also
When our families come for
a visit

Before Mother left this
world
I was able
To tell her about it
And it made her happy
To know it was
Being used
As I stood
And looked at it
I thought of Mother
And years of long ago

I went over
And touched it
As she had so many times
Then I left the Parlor
Before this
Sweet Remembrance of
Mother
Overflowed
Into tears

Only For A Time
April 19, 2006

I thought of you
This April morn
I thought of your precious
smile

Which lit up your face
The Last time I saw you

I remembered
That sweet little voice
That touched my heart so much
And I remembered
That little hurt sound
That I heard escape
Behind that precious smile
When I said
I had to leave

And then I remembered
The Last Words
I heard
In the distance of the phone
When I told the caretaker
To tell you
I Love You
You said - Thank You!
Thank You!

Words
That were often on your lips
In gratitude
For Everything

Then
December 13, 2005 came
And I received a call

In late evening
That the nurse
Checking upon you
Had asked
Mrs. Alma or Mrs. Sargent
Are you alright
I was told
You lifted your head
And said
I'm alright
I'm fine
Laid your head back down
And moments later
Slipped away

O Mama!
How I Miss You!

But I know
There will come a day
When I too
Will depart this earth

So
I have to remember
This Parting
Is not forever
But
Only For A Time

Tam
July 26, 2010
(most of poem was written
February 21, 2013)

My Mother
Went to Chicago
Many years ago
To visit her Aunt Elizabeth
While she was there
She went to see a friend
Mrs. Sarah Boston
Who had a little girl
Named - Tam

Tam
Was pretty indeed
And Mother told me
That she could really
Play the piano

Over the years
Even after
Ms. Sarah
Had departed this earth
Whenever Tam
Would come to visit her
relatives
She would try to come by
And see Mother

I believe Mother told me once
That she even came up
From New Orleans
A 4-hour drive
To the Alexandria and Pineville area
Just to visit her
I was really touched
But
I was even more touched
For at Mother's Wake Service
Tam happened to be
In New Orleans
And she came up
To tell her friend
Goodbye

Martha and Martha and Mary

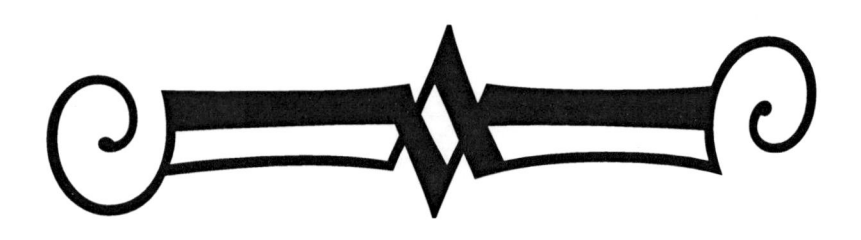

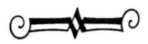

Martha and Martha and Mary
July 29, 2010

In the First Century A.D.
There was a Martha
Who prepared
A great dinner
For Jesus

She had a sister
Named Mary
Who greeted Jesus
When He came
And then
Sat at His feet
To listen
To His Golden Words

Now in this 21st Century
In this year of 2010
On this Feast day of St. Martha
I am thinking
Of another Martha
That was
So special to me
She was my Aunt
My very dear dear
Aunt Martha

She too
Had a sister
Who was her twin
And her name was Mary
They were my Aunts
But the one
Named Mary
I never met
For she left this world
When she was around eight years old

My dear Aunt Martha
Was retarded
And did not talk too much
But I am told
That Mary said
She would do
All the talking
For both of them

I'm sure she did
Until
God took her away

Before I was born
My Grandmother
And Aunt Martha
Came to live with my parents
And I have pictures

Of Aunt Martha holding me
When I was
Around 3 weeks old

All thru my life
She has been with us
And she became
Ever so dear
To my heart

Some years ago
After I entered
Religious Life
I asked God
To grant me
Two Favors
In her regard
Though she was around 80
Or almost
She had not been baptized
So I prayed
That God would grant
That she be baptized

Then
Next I requested
That God would grant me
The Favor
Of letting her somehow
Merit more and more
So that she could win
A very very beautiful place

In Heaven

My Beautiful God
My Precious Sacred Heart
Granted me
These Two Favors

My Mother
Was nearly 90 herself
But she made the
arrangements
And my dear Aunt Martha
Was baptized
And became a member
Of the
Wesley United Methodist
Church
That was down the street
And where my Father
Had been a member

My Mother was Baptist
And most of my people

Mother was very pleased
And told me
Aunt Martha
Really looked nice

How grateful I was
To My God for this Favor

Not too long after this
Mother's health
Began to fail
More and more

And
To our Amazement
Aunt Martha
Shone Forth
And was able to help her
More and more

If she needed an arm
To lean on
To help her
Get around the house
Aunt Martha
Was glad to give her one
She began doing
A number of things
Around the house to help out
Making the bed - sweeping the floor
Washing dishes after meals
Trying to keep the kitchen neat
She even learned
How to push
The one-minute button
On the microwave
To heat their food!

She often got the mail
Went to the door
When someone came
And many times a day
She would bring Mother
A glass of water
Or a cold drink
And more often
Than it should have been
She would also bring her
A piece of cake
Or a few cookies

When the Home Health
People came
Since Aunt Martha
Was talking a little more - in her later years
Especially to Mother
She would tell them
That Mother
Had too much cake
Or too many cookies
But she never mentioned
How many she had too!
So in this manner
My Precious Sacred Heart
My Beautiful God
Granted me
The Second Favor
That I requested
Because I know

All these little acts
Of great love and kindness
That Aunt Martha has done
for Mother
Helped her
To merit
More and more

My dear dear
Aunt Martha
Departed this world
On Thanksgiving Day
November, 2008
And I believe
That My Precious Sacred
Heart
My Beautiful God
Has granted her
A very very beautiful
dwelling place
In His Kingdom
And I pray
That she has had
The Happiness
Of meeting her twin sister
Mary
And also
The Happiness
Of meeting
The Martha and Mary
Of Jesus' Time

Above: My Dear Parents,
Ruben and Alma Sargent

Right: My Dear Aunt,
Martha Potter

Part Five

Dr. Martin Luther King, Jr.

Way before my Time
Way beyond anything I can remember
There lived a man
that God called in a special way
Led him atop a mountain
And gave him a Mighty Mission.

A mission that would take him
many years to fulfill
A mission that would not be easy
A mission that would be filled
with many trials and tribulations
But, God promised to be with him
And give him all he would need
to accomplish this task.

This man of God was the Great Moses

His mission to go down to Egypt
And tell Pharaoh,
"Let My People Go"
And he was then to lead
This whole nation of God's people
Out of that Land

Twenty-two years ago
in my lifetime
There was another man
that God called in a special way
And gave him a Mighty Mission.

A mission that would take him
many years and even today
is not totally fulfilled
A mission that would not be easy
A mission that would be filled
with many trials and tribulations
But God was with him
And gave him all he needed
to accomplished the task
that was put before him

This man of God
Was the Great Dr. Martin
Luther King, Jr.
His mission
To break the bonds and
chains
of Segregation
that all Black men
may be Free
To Fight for Righteousness
And Justice for all people
in a Non-Violent way

This was his creed - his
strong belief
It caused him - to lose his
life

From my heart
I Thank You - Thank You -
Dr. King

FOR I AM FREE

A Calling
November 25, 2010

I just watched the Movie
Amazing Grace

Powerful Indeed!
It showed the struggle
Of
William Wilberforce
To have laws passed
That would abolish slavery
In the British Government
And his friend
William Pitt - who later
became Prime Minister
Also desired it
And encouraged and helped
him
Along the way

Wilberforce
Struggled and struggled
To get laws changed
It became
Such a part of his life
That his health
Was extremely affected
And after
15 years of this struggle
And still
It had not been
accomplished
He was
About to give up
For it had
Such a hold on him
That he could not

Sleep peacefully
But was bombarded
In his dreams
With the
Horrors of Slavery

When
He was at this point
According to the movie
The woman
He later married
Encouraged him
Not to Give Up!
He listened
And despite his ill health
He continued
The Struggle

God had given him
A Calling
Laid a Special Mission
A special cause
Upon his heart
Gave him
A special work
To do for Him

With
Amazing Grace
William Wilberforce
Persevered
He did not give up

Even when
It seemed - Hopeless
After the struggle
Of so many years
With Renewed
Encouragement
He continued!
Several more years
Passed by
And Finally!
He was
Victorious! Take courage
From William Wilberforce
And if God
Has called you
To do
A certain thing for Him
To Carry out
Some special mission
No matter
What the odds are
No matter
How bleak
It may look

STAND FIRM
TO YOUR CALLING!

Equiano
November 28, 2010

Equiano
Was in this movie
He had once been a slave
Now free
He was spending
His life
Trying to help
Free
Other slaves

According to the movie
He gathered much
information
And told
How they were treated
Equiano had once been like
a Prince
In his Land
Among his people
He turned over the
information
To Wilberforce

Equiano
Did not live
To see the Victory
But I pray

That he rejoiced
From the Eternal Shores

In a Decade or Two
December 3, 2010

In a decade or two
I may no longer be here

In a decade or two
My life on this earth
May truly be ended

Will I have carried out
The Mission
God gave me to do?

Will I have done
What I was destined to do
From All Eternity?

I pray so
That I may
Then be able
To depart
In Total Peace

I ask you
In a decade or two
Will you have carried out

The Mission
God gave you to do?

Will you have done
What you were destined to
do?

Most Importantly
Will you be ready
To meet
Your Creator
In a decade or two
Or Even Sooner?

Part Six

Warm Memories
of
Others
Who Touched My Life

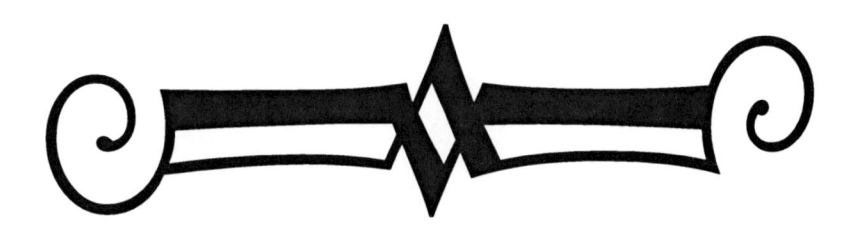

In the Year of 2010

Mr. Mike Grady
June 10, 2010

Mr. Grady
Came to Mass today
I had not seen him
In sometime

He used to come
Almost every Saturday
Along with
His lovely Mother

He always stays
After Mass
To say a rosary
And does it
So very devoutly

Whenever he can
He likes to come early
Before Mass

And spend
Some quiet time
Before the Blessed
Sacrament
He is a very prayerful person
And his countenance
Is very edifying
One day when he came
Mr. Grady wanted me
To ask all the Sisters
To pray
For a good friend of his
Who was going thru
A very difficult time
Due to the economic
conditions
Of our time
He had a deep and true
Concern for him and his
family
I assured him
Of our prayers

May God always bless
Mr. Grady
With a kind
And compassionate heart
And when he leaves this
world
May He show him
The Kindness and
Compassion

Of His Heart
And
Welcome him
Into His Kingdom

Truly Special
June 10, 2010

From time to time
I think of their Mother
Who was so special
To Mr. Grady
And his brother Tom
I remember too
The day I spoke to Tom
He talked about his Mother
And as I listened to him
What he said
Was very touching
And showed
His deep love for her

Some years ago
She was going to see about
A family member
Who was ill
And on the trip
She unexpectedly
Departed this world

In the midst of
Of
A great Act of love
And charity
God suddenly called her home
O! With What Great
Love and charity
Our Lord
Must have received her
When she left this world

I pray they all meet again someday
Upon the realms
Of Paradise

Mr. Grady's Family
January 30, 2011

On August 19, 2010
Mr. Grady and his brother
And their sister
And her children
Came to Mass

His sister Carol
And her family
Were visiting from Virginia
At some point
He had introduced me

And I spoke to them
For a few minutes
Then gave them
Some Sacred Heart badges
And a few other things

Later
After Mass
When I went outside
For a few moments
I found the children
Waiting patiently
For Mr. Grady and his brother
To say their rosary

It was then
That Little Rose - age 7
Spoke of Austin
She told me
He was 13
And that he was handicapped
I told her
He must be the source
Of lots of love
In the Family

I then told her
That I had
A retarded Aunt
Who had been

So very sweet

It has been
A real pleasure
Meeting
Some of Mr. Grady's Family
I pray
That God will bless them
And always give them
His special guidance thru life

⸻

Mr. Tom Grady
January 20, 2011

Mr. Grady has a brother
Named Tom
He comes to Mass
With him sometimes

One day
I got a chance
To talk to him
And it was most edifying
To listen to him

He was praying
And asking God
For a very special favor
But he was quite resigned

To accept
God's Will
If He did not grant it

What an example
Of a
True Christian Attitude!

I pray that God
Will some day
Grant him this favor
And may he someday
Grant him
The Favor
Of entering
Paradise

The Sacred Heart Bouquet
June 11, 2010

I arranged
A special bouquet
Worked on it
Late into the night
Because
My day had been
So busy
That there was
No other time to do it

But I didn't mind
And truly enjoyed it
For it was
To be given
To a very special someone
A special someone
That I was most grateful to
For all her help
In the Sacristy

So I chose
A very nice clear vase
And I filled it with water
Then I put in
Lovely carnations
Alstroemerias
That were rose colored
And in very full bloom
One stem was red and white
And so were
Some of the carnations
Except for three pure white ones
I put
Baby's breath here and there
And beautiful greens all about
Which included leather leaves
And one long green stem
That was different from the

rest
I placed it
Right up the middle
And this gave the bouquet
A nice height
I then finished it off
By placing
A pretty red bow
In the front
After this - I went to bed!

I do hope
That this special someone
Who is My Sacristy Angel
Will be wonderfully
surprised
And truly love this
Sacred Heart Bouquet
That I have
So lovingly
Tried to arrange
To show her
My Gratitude
For all her kindness to me

P.S.
This Bouquet
Was Given to Isabel Crunk
On
The Feast of the Sacred
Heart
June 11, 2010

The Thank You Note
June 11, 2010

My Dear Isabel
I just want to say
That I wish you
A very happy
Sacred Heart Feast day

And most of all
I want to say
Thank you! Thank you!
For all the help
You have given me
In the Sacristy
During these busy days
From preparing
For the Feast of Corpus
Christi
Thru the
Sacred Heart Triduum

May this
Sacred Heart Bouquet
And the Mass
you will be included in
tonight
For the
Feast of the Sacred Heart
Help to express

My deep gratitude

May God Forever Bless You
For your kindness to me
And may
The Sacred Heart
One day
Show you the depth of His
Kindness
In Paradise

Love,
Sister Mary of the Sacred
Heart

My Sacristy Angel
October 24, 2010

On Sundays
After Benediction
I have
A special helper
Who puts the candles out
And then helps me
To clear the Altar
Of everything that is used
for Benediction
We then
Have to change
The Altar cloth
To the weekday one
Then change the Tabernacle
veil
And take down
The Sunday candelabras
After that
The Morning Mass
Preparations
Have to be done
Including laying out the
vestments
For Father
On the vestment press
Which is a special counter
top
For that purpose

If I have to leave
For a few minutes
This special helper
Continues on quietly
And very efficiently
Getting things done
For she has been helping me
For several years now
And knows
Where most things are kept

This special helper
Is my Dear Isabel Crunk
Who was one of those
That rescued me

During Holy Week
Now
She is not only
A special helper
But
She has truly become
My Sacristy Angel

May the Sacred Heart
someday
Lift her up
To dwell with Him Forever
In the presence
Of His Angels

༺═╬═༻

The Sacristy Helpers
October 24, 2010

Some years ago
When I was not
In the Sacristy
For some months
But was working
In another area
For a short while
The Sister taking care of it
Became ill
And it was
Holy Week!
The Very Busiest Week
Of the year!
So I was summoned
To come to
The Rescue!

In God's Great Goodness
And Kindness
Emmanuella
Rafaela
And Isabel
Were making
Their usual
Holy Week Retreat here
with us
And when
They discovered my situation
They came to
My Rescue!
For so much
Had to be done
And there was only
A few days
To do it
So they set to work
Helping me
All during the day
And even late
Into the night
And together
Everything got done
And went quite well

I believe
After this
They had a much deeper
appreciation
Of all that is done
In their parishes
To make
Their services so beautiful
For they were amazed
At all the work
That had to be done
For Special Times

We had
A Mass said for them
In gratitude
And I will be
Forever Thankful
For all the help
They gave me
During that Holy Week

They did not have
Too much of a Retreat
But I pray
That one day
In the Land of Paradise
That the Sacred Heart will grant
Emmanuella
Rafaela

And Isabel
Treasures Untold
And so many special blessings
And wonderful surprises
For this Act of Love for Him
And this
Great Generosity of Help!

Emmanuella's Gift

My Dear Emmanuella
Attended
Our Thanksgiving Day Mass
This morning

I was glad to see her
And quite a number of people
That had come
To offer up
Thanks to God
On this day set aside
Specially
By Our Country

Around a week ago
I found out
That her dear Mother
Mrs. Genera Fabre Medina

Had died
On November 16, 2008

After we arranged
To have a Mass said for her
On the Feast of Christ the King
Emmanuella and I
Had a most wonderful
And very inspiring little talk

We spoke of her Mother
And she told me
How beautifully
Mrs. Medina had accepted
Her sufferings
In union
With Jesus on the Cross
Emmanuella said
That she had now come
To a much deeper understanding
Of the Cross
As she spent
These last months
With her Mother

God
In His great goodness
And kindness
Granted Mrs. Medina
The Wonderful Blessing

Of celebrating
Her 60th Wedding Anniversary
The end of October - 2008
What a statement
Of Love and Marriage Commitment
In our time

As she spoke
The love for her Mother
And her Father too
Shone thru her words
And so precious to me
Was when Emmanuella said
That when her Mother
Could not speak
She would whisper
Ejaculations
In her ear
So that she could
Lift them up
To God
How beautiful!

Before Emmanuella left that day
I gave her
A little gift
That really touched her heart
And I told her
How I came about it

Sometime after
She asked me
To set it down
In writing
So I will now relate
How I came about
Emmanuella's Gift

This year
On September 11, 2008
About 9:30 pm
Sister Mary Jozefa
Kowalewski
Died
She was our former Superior
Of many years
And oftentimes
Was still called
Mother Jozefa
Emmanuella
Has been a long time friend
Of our Monastery
And Mother Jozefa
Was very special to her

When I called
To tell her
She informed me
That her Mother was very ill
Therefore
She was not able to come

To the Funeral Services
Later
She told me
How she longed to come
But just could not

Mrs. Ferris
Another long-time friend
Of our Monastery
Was in Virginia at the time
And when I spoke to her
She asked me
To please save her
Some little memento
Mother gathered
Several things
And said
She could have her choice

I had these items
In the Sacristy
Where I work
But when I went on Retreat
For a week
October 20th - 26th
I decided
To take these items
To my room
Until Mr. and Mrs. Ferris
could come

After my Retreat

I brought them back
To the Sacristy
And not long after that
Mr. and Mrs. Ferris
Came to our Chapel
For Mass
Afterwards
They made their choice

One thing Mrs. Ferris chose
Was a most unusual picture
Of St. Joseph with Jesus
In his Carpenter Shop
Mother Jozefa
Loved St. Joseph
Both of them
Also got
One of her rosaries
And Mr. Ferris
Liked a special key chain
That had our 7 Visitation
Martyrs
Of Spain on it
I also gave them
A memorial card
That had her picture on it
They were quite pleased
With these items
And I was glad

Then one day
Shortly after this

When I was in my room
I discovered
That I had forgotten
The Cross
I intended especially
To give to Mrs. Ferris

I took it back
To the Sacristy
And I wondered
Who I could give it to
But as I thought over it
And the way
I had forgotten it
In my room
It seemed to me
That God had
Someone Special
In mind

So I decided
To let it stay
On the counter
Along with a memorial card
That had
Mother Jozefa's picture on it
That I somehow
Also happened to have

My thought
Was to let them both
Remain there

132

Until God
Would let me know
In some way
The Special Person
He had destined this for

As Emmanuella
Spoke so beautifully
Of Jesus on the Cross
I knew
That she was the one
That God had chosen
To receive
This Special Gift

May it always be
A special treasure to her
And may

The Sweet Holy Spirit
Who she loves so dearly
Keep her safe
As He guides her
Thru this life
And when it's time
For her to depart
This world
May He lift her
Upon His wings
And let her
Soar
To Paradise

Rafaela
November 20, 2010

Today
November 20th
2010
Our Community
Is celebrating
The Feast of the Presentation
Of Our Lady
In the Temple
Each year
On this Feast
We renew our Vows
The actual day
Should be November 21st
But this year
That happens to be
The Last Sunday of the
Church Year
And therefore
The Feast of Christ the King

At some point
I happened to notice
That Rafaela had come
Into the Chapel
I was glad to see her
For she had not been here
In a while

I was also glad
That she happened to come
On this special day
For she enjoys being with us
On special occasions

When Mass was over
I went out to greet her
And to give her
A little package
That I had for her

Later
In the morning
We got a chance
To have
A pleasant little chat

She told me
A little about
How she became Catholic
She is from South Korea
And said
When she was in about
The Fourth Grade
She stopped by a Church
While she was out walking
With a friend
She wanted
To go to Confession
This apparently led her
Into deep inquiries

About the Faith
For eventually
She joined the Catholic
Church

She went on to tell me
About her recent trip to
France
Which she enjoyed very
much
And I thanked her
For the little gift
That she brought me from
there

We spoke a few minutes
more
Then our pleasant little chat
ended
And we said
Goodbye

Ms. Pecolia Brown
June 20, 2010

Ms. Pecolia
Came to bring us something
today
I had been thinking about
her

This past week

She is a very gracious lady
And seems to be
Full of Life

She stopped at our
Monastery
One day
To inquire
If we had anyone
Who was deaf
I told her we did
But that this Sister
Had been a religious
For many years
And we had no problem
Communicating with her
That's how
I came to meet her
A year or 2 ago

Since then
Every now and then
She brings us
A very nice treat
Like this Deluxe Chocolate
Cake
And we have
A little chat for a few
minutes

She likes
To bring a few friends along
sometime
And likes me to tell them
Something about
Our Religious Way of Life
And how I came to be a nun
She spoke of it being rare
For them
To go to a Monastery
And I don't think any
Had ever met
A Black Nun

I enjoy talking to her
And her friends
And I try to answer
Their questions
About Our Life

Today
She brought a nice couple
And a man and his daughter
Whose name was Dallas
And she was 6 years old
And very cute
And quite well-mannered
As they spoke

I admire
Ms. Pecolia and
The friends she brings

We are of very different
faiths
Neither she nor her friends
Bring any paper books and
so forth
Or try to persuade me
To their religion
They are respectful of mine
And I try to be respectful of
theirs

She was wearing
A dress today mostly red
And she had on
A white Jacket over it
She really looked nice
And when I opened the
door
She greeted me
With her cheery smile.

May God Bless them All!

The Flower Lady
June 21, 2010

From time to time
There is a lady
That will stop by
Our Monastery

Ring the door-bell
And surprise us
With several bunches
Of beautiful flowers

She usually comes
On a Saturday
And I set to work
Arranging them into
bouquets
For Sunday Mass

Recently
She brought us
Some very beautiful roses
We had just celebrated
The Feast of the Sacred
Heart
So the Chapel already had
Several arrangements for the
Feast

We would be celebrating
The Immaculate Heart of
Mary
The next day
And she wanted
To honor her specially
So I got
Two nice sized vases
And arranged these flowers
We have

A lovely statue
Of the Immaculate Heart of
Mary
In a niche on the hallway
I placed a vase
On each side of her

A picture was taken of it
For it was within the cloister
And dropped in with a
Thank You Note
The Flower Lady
Was touched even to tears
And I told her
That I thought
Our Lady was very pleased
With the Roses
She gave her

May Our Lady
Place her blessing upon her
For this Special Gift

And may God grant
Terri Pearson
The sweet Flower Lady
His Special Blessings too
For all the Flowers
She has brought
To beautify
The Chapel

Deacon Mobley's Beautiful Gesture
June 24, 2010

On the First Sunday
Of every month
Deacon Michael Mobley
Comes for Benediction
It is a big help
To Father Fallon
Who comes
The other Sundays of the
month
But has a very busy schedule
And also a prison ministry

At some point
I realized
That the First Sunday
In July
Would be
July 4th
Our Nation's Birthday
And a
National Holiday
A Great Day of Celebration
Across the Country

Deacon Mobley
Has been giving us

Benediction
For several years
But he has been coming
To our Monastery
For many years
And was a very
Faithful Member
Of the Guard of Honor
For all the years
That we conducted it

I remember him
Telling me
That it took him
About an hour
To get from his house
To St. Stephen the Martyr
Church
Where he is a
Full-time Deacon
He went on
To tell me
That whenever
He would come
For the Guard of Honor
meetings
Or for Benediction
In the afternoon
He stays
At the Church
Until it is time
To come here

Sometimes
That means leaving his
house
Around 7 or 7:30 am in the
morning
And not returning
Until around 7:30 pm in the
evening
For it takes him
About one and a half
From the Monastery
Thinking over this Holiday
I could see
That this would take up
His entire day
Because the Deacon
Told me he had
The 8:30 Mass at St.
Stephen's

So I spoke to Mother
About it
And I was given permission
To call him
And tell him
To enjoy the day
With his family
When I spoke to him
He had been
So committed
To fulfilling this special duty
That he had not realized

That the First Sunday
Was on the 4th of July

Then he said to me
Are you sure
For it's a privilege
Coming for Benediction
I told him
We would be celebrating
The 4th
In our Monastic Way
And we certainly
Wanted him
To celebrate it with his
Family
Again he wanted to be sure
It was okay
Because he was still
Willing to come
I assured him again
And he was quite appreciative

But Oh!
I thought
What kindness, generosity and fidelity
And what
A truly special love
He must have for us

And most of all

What a truly special love
He must have for God
Which shines thru
When he is
In the Presence
Of the Blessed Sacrament

May Our Dear Lord
Reward him greatly
When he enters
The Golden Gates
Of Paradise

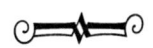

―――

Mary, The Deacon's Wife
September 16, 2011

Every now and then
Mary
Deacon Mobley's wife
Gets a chance
To come with him
It is always good
To see her

She too
Likes to spend
Some quiet time in prayer
Before the Blessed Sacrament

And it is most edifying to me
For it is always wonderful
To see people
Spend special time with God

We really enjoy
Having a chat with her
If there is
Some special celebration
And everyone is invited
To go to the Parlor
Afterwards

On one of these
Special Occasions
That took place in August
We happened to find out
That it was
Her Birthday!
So we gave her
A Great Big Piece
Of Chocolate Cake!
To take home!

P.S.
One time
The Deacon
Spoke about his life
And he mentioned
That he had
A very beautiful wife

And how
She had helped
To bring about
Some wonderful changes
In his life

I thought
She is truly beautiful
And very understanding
Of the Deacon's Vocation
Which I believe
Brings down
Many special blessings
Upon their Marriage

May God Forever
Increase their love
And shower them
With His special blessings
And may He someday
Lift their souls
And let them
Soar to Heaven

Mr. Higgens
June 26, 2010

Mr. Higgens
Was our plumber
For many years

At the Monastery

He is truly a person
That loves his Profession
When he came
To fix problems
He would go
Into great detail
And tell you
All about it
He would show you
The different parts
He might be replacing
And explain them to you
As I said
He really loves his job

Some years passed
And
A little bundle of Joy
Came into the life
Of Mr. Higgens
And his lovely wife
That bundle of Joy
Was named - Crystal
And of course
She was just as cute
And precious
As she could be

They made
A special request

And what a delight it was
To have her Baptized
In our Chapel

I believe it was Easter - 2009
When they all came for
Mass
My! My!
Crystal had really grown!
No longer
A babe in arms
But now about 10 years old

I know
They love her dearly
And I pray
That God will bless them all
And keep them
Safe in his loving care

⚜

Mr. Higgens' Father
June 27, 2010

Mr. Higgens' Father
Mr. Robert Higgens
Was an unofficial
Guard of Honor member
He loved to come
When he could
And we really enjoyed

Having him at the meeting
He was wonderful

In March - 2008
Mr. Higgens departed this world
I pray that
The Sacred Heart
Whom the
Guard of Honor Group Honors
Was there
To greet him
When he opened his eyes
And make him
An official member
Of Paradise

⚜

Mr. Lancour
June 27, 2010

A few days ago
I was very touched
By the great respect
And reverence
That Mr. Lancour
Showed to the Blessed Sacrament

His dear wife

Mrs. Sybil Lancour
Needs a special glucose-free host
They bring it in a pix
And place it on the altar
For Father to consecrate
During Mass
That she may be able
To receive Holy Communion

After Mass today
Mr. Lancour
Set out to retrieve the pix
As he approached the Sanctuary
He stood to one side
And made a little reverent bow
Then
When He came to the Center
And was facing the Tabernacle
He made
A very reverent genuflection
And bowed his head
For a moment of prayer
Then he stepped into the Sanctuary
Retrieved the pix
Made another little bow

Towards the Tabernacle
Stepped down
From the Sanctuary
And when he came again
To the center
And was facing the
Tabernacle
He again made another
Prayerful genuflection
I really was touched
By the love and honor
And reverence
That he showed Our Lord
How pleasing this must be
To the Heart of God!

Mrs. Sybil Lancour's Hobby
June 27, 2010

Once
When we were having
A Special Celebration
And the people
Could join us in the parlor
I had
A very enjoyable
conversation
With Mrs. Sybil Lancour
She told me

That she made quilts
And as I listened to her
She seemed to have
A special joy and love
In making them
I do know
They can truly be
A most beautiful work of art
And when each stitch
Is filled with love
They become a treasure
That is more precious than
gold

May God Bless her always
And this hobby of hers
That fills others
With so much joy and
happiness

The Beautiful Ceremony
June 27, 2010

A few years ago
Mr. and Mrs. Druzik
Celebrated
Their 50th Wedding
Anniversary

In our Chapel
They Renewed
Their Wedding Vows
And while they did so
Mrs. Druzik
Looked upon Mr. Druzik
With such a look of love
That it was
Touching to the heart
Their Rings
Had been placed
Upon
A golden tray
Before Mass
And Father Mendes
Carried out everything
So wonderfully special

It was really
A Beautiful Ceremony!

Sunday Best
July 14, 2010

When I was growing up
People sat aside
Special attire
To be used
Only on Sunday
Or some very special

occasion
And especially
When you were
Going to Church

I remember having
Nice Sunday dresses
Nice Sunday shoes
Hats
Purses
And little white gloves
You really wanted
To look your best
When you went to Church

I thought of this
When I remembered a day
That I happened
To compliment
Mr. and Mrs. Steven Druzik
On how nice they looked
They told me
They like to wear
Their
Sunday Best to Church
It then came to me
That the Bible does speak
Of wearing
Holy Attire

How pleased God must be
When He looks down and

sees
Mr. and Mrs. Druzik
Wearing
Their Sunday Best
Just For Him!

The Family Breakfast
October 16, 2010

One Sunday
Mr. and Mrs. Druzik
Told me something
That was good to hear
They said
Their Family
Gather on Sunday Mornings
At their home
And they have
A Family Breakfast

How wonderful!
And how much better
The world would be
If more people
Followed their example
And had
A Family Breakfast

The Special Kindness
October 17, 2010

Mr. and Mrs. Druzik's
daughter
Stephanie
And her husband Edward
Often come
To our Chapel
For Mass too

They have
A vegetable garden
And sometimes
Bring us
Some of their
Good - fresh vegetables
When I give them
To Sister Cook
A big smile
Comes upon her face

We really do enjoy them
And are most grateful
For their Special Kindness
to us

May God Bless them
For their goodness
In sharing with their
neighbors

The Candle Lighter
July 17, 2010

The Candle-Lighter
Came to my aid
In this year of 2010
And also last year
In 2009
I was very grateful

For many years
I have used
A small stool
To lift me up
To perform
This precious little duty

It is
A small thing to do
But its meaning
Is Overwhelming
And affects
The whole world
And not only
The whole world
But every generation
That has been
That is
And
That will be

This little precious duty
Is lighting
The Paschal Candle
Our symbol
For
The Resurrection of Our
Lord Jesus Christ
And His being
The Light of the World
His Victorious Triumph over
sin and death
And His reopening
The Gates of Paradise
That we may one day
Receive Eternal Life

I have been pleased
To carry out this little duty
For so many years
But I was grateful
To the Candle-Lighter
Who wanted to save me
From having
To get upon the stool
By this kind Act of Charity

May God Bless
Mr. Druzik
For this
Special Act of Kindness
And

May the Light of this world
Someday grant him
The Light of His Face
Forever

⊙━━◆━━⊙

Precious Rewards
February 20, 2011

Yesterday
Which was
February 19, 2011
Mr. Druzik
Stayed after Mass
To fix a shelf for me
In the Sacristy

When he finished
I asked him
How much
Did we owe him
He said - just a prayer

He then
Went on to tell me
That both his Father
And his Grandfather
Had been quite exceptional
His Father
Had been a very good bricklayer
And his Grandfather
Worked with wood
They were very generous
men
And they instilled in him
That all work
That is done for the Church
Is work done for God
And therefore
There is No Charge!
He said
That he
And his Father
And his Grandfather
Have never accepted
Anything
For work done
For the Church

I told him
That was something
Wonderful to hear
And it was most edifying

As he spoke of his Father
And his Grandfather
I believe he became
A little misty-eyed
And his voice conveyed
A very deep love for them

I believe

The hearts
Of his Father and
Grandfather
Must have been
Very pleased
To know
That Mr. Druzik
Was following
The Wonderful Example
Of their generosity
To the Church
And so many others

I am sure
Our Lord was pleased
With all they did
To honor Him
And was most pleased
To give them
Their everlasting - Precious
Rewards

◦═◆═◦

Mr. and Mrs. John Ribblett
July 18, 2010

Mr. and Mrs. Ribblett
Are a nice couple
That comes to
Sunday Mass

In our Chapel

They greet me
With a warm smile
And
Good Morning Sister

One day
Mr. Ribblett
Wanted to know
If we would be interested
In some shawls
I checked with Mother
And not long afterwards
Mrs. Ribblett
Gave us a bunch
Of beautiful black shawls
That she had made

We were very grateful to them
For this kindness
And for all their generosity
To us
Since they have been
Coming to our Chapel

May God Bless them
Abundantly

◦═◆═◦

Kroger's Flower Shop
July 18, 2010

I often go to Kroger's
To get flowers
For the Chapel
Especially
For Big Feast Days
They have
A very wonderful variety
And I really enjoy
Shopping there.

Joyce and Marcell
The ladies that work there
Are always
So nice and helpful
They really make
Beautiful arrangements
And are very busy
For Mother's Day
High-school proms
Valentine's Day
And other special days
During the year
Sometimes
They give me
Helpful hints in making my
arrangements
And I am so very grateful to
them

May God Always bless them
And all the people that work
In this
Wonderful Kroger Store of
Snellville

Herman and Zeek
July 19, 2010

I saw someone today
That reminded me of
Herman

Herman worked for
A construction company
Owned by Mr. Vick
Mr. Vick and his son Buddy
Did a lot of jobs
Around our Monastery
Over the years
Renovations
Additions
Installing new shrines
All sorts of things
That have helped our
Monastery
Have its present beauty
That is how
We came to know
Herman and Zeek

Herman
Was always here
On these different jobs
And it didn't seem like
There was anything
He could not do
Mother Jozefa Kowalewski
Said he was
A genius
He really knew a lot
About many things
He has done
All sorts of jobs
To help us
Even assisting
With our Christmas decorations
Zeek
Was always
Right there to help him
In these different jobs

One day
When Zeek was outside
But with a view
Of the Sacristy window
He saw me ironing
Without a light
I often do this
Because I can see
Wrinkles much better

So from then on
To Zeek
I was the Sister
Who liked to iron
In the dark

After several years
Of coming to the Monastery
Zeek retired
He thought
It was time
To take it easy
He is probably
Stretched out
In a lawn chair
Or
Gone Fishing!

It's been sometime
Since I have seen Herman
He too may be retired now

At some point
When Herman was working here
And rushing about
Here and there
I was told
That he was in his sixties
I couldn't believe it!
I thought
He was in his forties

150

Especially
Since he moved about
Like he was 16!

May God Bless All of them
And help them
On their journey
To Eternity

Sophia's Cake
July 19, 2010

The doorbell rang
And someone went to answer
It was our neighbor
Who lived in the beautiful house
Across the street
Mrs. Sophia Clanton
She had come
To bring us
A special treat
A scrumptious looking chocolate cake

We had it for dessert
At dinner
It was so light and moist
And just

Absolutely Delicious!

Mr. Frank Lentini
October 15, 2006

Mr. Frank Lentini
Passed away
On October 11, 2006
He was one of our neighbors

I did not know him well
But for some years
From time to time
He attended Mass at our Monastery
Along with his nice wife
Flora
And his very lovely daughter
Sophia

Around 2 or 3 years ago
His daughter bought
The beautiful new house
Across the street from us
Therefore
We saw them more often
And eventually
Mr. and Mrs. Lentini came
to live there
Sophia and her new

husband - Steven Clanton
Fixed a section of their
home
Into a quaint
Private apartment for them
With its own private entrance
They thought
It would be a good idea
For her parents
To be near them
In their later years
And besides
They would have the special joy
Of a new grand-baby
For Sophia
Was expecting her first child

I remember
How happy
They were with the News
And how happy
We all were for them
At the Monastery
All of them
Were beaming
And filled with excitement

Later
On one trip to the doctor
They found out

It was going to be
A Boy!
This made for more excitement!

It was
A special happiness
Watching their happiness

What I remember in particular
Is the time
Mr. Lentini spoke to me
A few moments
Near the Chapel gates
His voice
And his words
Were filled with love
As he spoke of his daughter
Sophia
And how Special
She was to him
It was quite touching

It was in the Summer
In the month of August
I never suspected
That he would be gone
At the beginning of Fall

But God
Has called him Home

And in His Wisdom
He knows
What is Best

Sophia and Mrs. Lentini
And their Family
Can take consolation
In knowing
How much he loved them
And
In all the wonderful things
They have found out
Since he left this world
For so many people
Have stepped forward
And said
How wonderful Mr. Lentini was
And how helpful he had been to them

I am sure
God will reward him
With treasures untold
Which he will be waiting
To share with them
When they reach
The other side

Mrs. Attridge and The Nice Lady
July 24, 2010

One First Friday
When Mrs. Attridge
Came to the 7:30 pm Mass
In honor of the Sacred Heart
I happened to be
Near the door
When she came in

We exchanged greetings
And as we did so
I then noticed
That someone was with her
I barely glimpsed the person
Because she was behind her
I believe
It was then
That I made the comment
Oh! You have A Nice Lady with you!
Mrs. Attridge smiled
And told me
That was her daughter
I had to smile too
For now
Getting a full view of her

I could see
That it was her daughter -
Gillian
That had come to Mass with her
A number of times

Now
She was almost grown up
How time
Truly does fly

P.S.
On December 8, 2010
Mrs. Attridge
And her daughter Gillian
The Nice Lady
Came to Mass

I got a chance
To have
A pleasant Little visit
With her
She is in college now
And also working
Therefore
She is quite busy
She has 2 more years
And hopes to go into
International Business

May God

Grant her
Her Dream
And bless and help
The Nice Lady
Forever

My Precious Holy Bible
July 24, 2010

As I held
My Precious Holy Bible
My eye
Fell upon the name
That was engraved
On the front cover
Kimberly Dinecola

My memory
Brought to mind
How I came
To have this Precious Book

I was looking for a Bible
That was not too large
To carry with me
When I entered Religious Life
The lady
At a bookstore
In Baton Rouge

Told me
That she could give me
A good discount
On a particular Bible
They had
It was very nice
Black and the pages
Were trimmed in gold
Someone
Had planned on buying it
And had requested
To have their name engraved
But
For some reason
Did not purchase it
After the name
Had been put on it

I liked it very much
And the price was Just Right
That was around 20 years ago
It is now
Somewhat worn
And the pages
Are no longer
Trimmed in gold
But it is still
So very Precious to me
For the Words of God
Are Eternal

Today
And other times
Over the years
When I look down
At the front cover
And see
Kimberly Dinecola
Inscribed in gold
I say a prayer for her

May God bless
And help her Always
And may we one day
Finally meet
In His Kingdom

The Hidden Talent
July 25, 2010

The doorbell rang
And I answered it
To my surprise
It was Mrs. Ferris

I had not seen her in a while
So it was
A most pleasant surprise
We chatted a few minutes
Then she told me

The purpose of her visit
She had come to bring back
A couple of wooden chairs
That she and her husband
Had refurbished for us

I was really surprised now!
Because
I had no idea
They did this kind of work
I had no idea
They had
This Beautiful Hidden
Talent!

Do you have
Any hidden talents?
If you do
Then let them
Shine forth for God
Be it just a smile
A few kind words
To lift a heart
And brighten someone's day

God will surely bless you
For using the Gift
He gave you

Mr. and Mrs. Raymond Ferris
August 9, 2009

Today
I heard
Some wonderful news
Mrs. Vickie Ferris
Told me
That she and her husband
Mr. Raymond Ferris
Would be celebrating
Their 50th Wedding
Anniversary
The actual date
Is August 18, 2009
But they are having
Their Big Celebration
On August 15, 2009

This was really wonderful to hear
For in the Society
That we live in today
There are many
Who will not have
This unique honor
Of celebrating
Their Golden Jubilee
Because of the

Breakdown
In Marriage Commitment
And so much re-marriage
Even multiple times
Therefore
There are not too many
Who will be able
To reach 50 years
With the same spouse
And know the joy
Of
A Golden Jubilee

But I am so happy
That Mr. and Mrs. Ferris
Will have this
Unique Honor

They have come
To our Chapel
For many years
And I am
Always glad to see them

I remember
When they first began to come
They reminded me
Of High School couples
Who are
So In Love
And want to be

Constantly together
And often
You will see these couples
Wearing
Matching shirts
Or sweaters
Which is
What I noticed
That the Ferris' did
From time to time
They seemed
To love being together
And it was warming
To my heart

Occasionally
Their daughter Melissa
Attends Mass here
It is always nice
To see her
I remember
When her son was small
How we watched him grow
Over the years
And later
To her surprise
And our delight
Little Faith
Came along
A new bundle of joy
To touch our lives

Eventually
As the years passed by
We came to know
Mrs. Ferris' Father
Who came
To live with them
He was in his nineties
And they really took
Loving care of him
Until it was time for him
To depart this earth
For the
Realm Beyond

May God always bless
Mr. and Mrs. Ferris
And their Family
And someday
Bring all of them
To the
Land of Heaven
In the Realm Beyond

⁓═╬═⁓

Tara
July 27, 2010

Tara
When it comes to mind
We think of
Gone With The Wind

We think of
That beautiful plantation
home
And grounds
And Scarlett O'Hara
Frolicking About
Especially
In the days
Of her youth

But the Tara
I am speaking of now
Is someone
I met briefly
And found her a joy
She is Sister Mary Regina's
niece
And she came to visit her

She too is beautiful
And one day
I saw a picture of her home
Though it was not like
Scarlett's
It certainly
Was very beautiful

Her Sister
Who is an airline pilot
Came
A little later

158

They all had
A really wonderful
Little visit

Tara and her sister
Had taken some time out
Of their busy schedule
To come and see
Their dear Aunt
For it had been a while
So they decided
To make
A Quick Trip

I know this must have touched
And warmed
Sister Mary Regina's heart
And I thought
What a precious way
For them to express
Their love and care
For their Aunt

P.S.:
Later
After their visit
When Sister spoke of it
I could tell
They have captured
Special Places
In her heart

A Beautiful Act of Charity
July 27, 2010

At Recreation
Sister Mary Regina
Spoke of
A Most
Beautiful Act of Charity

An elderly person
Was seeking a job
And her brother
Came to know of it
He could not hire this person
But Sister Mary Regina said
Every month
Her brother
Sent a check
To help this person
For years

I believe
When he reaches Eternity
He will find
A most precious reward
For this
Beautiful Act of Charity

Mr. Kevin Henderson
August 2, 2010

Mr. Henderson
Is a nice young man
That works in the bank
That is located
Inside of Publix
One of the large food stores
In our area
One day
When I came in
To get some bread
And a few other things
Mr. Henderson
Happened to be
In the vicinity of the front door
He said
Excuse me please
Are you a nun
I said yes
I don't know
If he had ever seen a nun
But somehow
We got around to the fact
That he surely
Had never seen
A black Nun!

I told him
It was not unusual
For someone
To come up to me
Or any of our sisters
If they happen to be out
And tell us
They have not seen Nuns
In a long time
And some will say
Not since their school days

I must admit
That one time
I was a little startled
When I happened to be
In a Drug Store
In Baton Rouge
And came upon
Some teenagers
One young man
Had a big smile
And said
I thought Nuns
Were just in the movies
I didn't know
They were
For Real!
I informed him
I was truly
A Real Nun
And we really do exist

We spoke
For a few more minutes
And I went on
To tell Mr. Henderson
A little about
Our Way of Life
He listened attentively
And was most respectful

I then said goodbye
And did my shopping

May God Forever Bless
Mr. Henderson

Kelon's Joy
January 16, 2011

On January 6, 2011
I went into Publix
To get some milk
I had not been in the store
In quite some time

When I went in
To my surprise
I saw Mr. Henderson
We talked
For a few minutes

And I asked him
About his Christmas
And told him
That our decorations
Were still up
Because our Christmas
Season
Lasts a long time
That is
Several weeks
According to the Church
Calendar

He told me
His decorations
Were still up too
Because
His three-year old son
Kelon
Loved them so

May God always
Fill the hearts
Of Mr. Henderson
His wife Tonya
And Kelon
With A
Special Christmas Joy

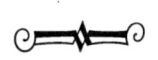

Mr. and Mrs. Eisenberg
August 4, 2010

Mr. and Mrs. Eisenberg
Are a couple
That come to Mass
At our Chapel sometimes

They are very devout
And really strive to live
A deep Christian Life

They try to see
And do God's will
In their daily lives
And they try to accept
Whatever He sends
Putting all their trust and confidence
In His loving care

May God some day
Reward
Mr. Howard Eisenberg
And his wife Catalina
With the Joys of Heaven
Forever!

Ena Neblett
August 5, 2010

Ena
Is a beautiful lady
From one of the
Caribbean Islands
She comes to our Chapel sometimes
But it has been quite a while
Since I have seen her
I wondered
If she had moved

She worked
In the medical field
And also
For a time
Had a ceramic shop
She and her husband
Donated us
A somewhat unusual cross
And a very nice statue
Of Saint Francis of Assisi
The cross
Is out on the grounds
And St. Francis
Is near
Located under the shade
Of some cool pine trees
And where we can see him
As we go
To and fro thru the house
We were very grateful

For this donation

One of the last times
That I talked to Ena
She told me
That she was working
At a Hospice Facility
She spoke of how
She really loved
Caring for those
Nearing the End
Of Life's Journey
And she called them
Her Angels

May God Forever bless her
For all her love and care and kindness
In this
Beautiful Work of God!
And may He someday
Send these
Angels of her heart
To fetch her and bring her
to Heaven
When her Life's Journey
Has come to an end

Spending Time with the Lord
August 8, 2010

Many of us
Go to Church on Sunday
To worship
And adore Our Lord
To Thank Him
For His goodness to us
And to ask His help
In our needs
In our troubles and trials
Then Monday comes
And our busy schedule
Starts all over again
By the end of the day
We are so tired
And exhausted
That we wonder
If we can even
Say our Night Prayers
And it is like this
Most of the week
A few manage
To get to Mass
Or some other service
Another time or two
In the week
And this is good

It is very good
And wonderful to see
All those
Who can make it to Mass
Every day or almost every
day

It is also
Wonderful to see
Those who come
During the day
To make
Little visits
To Our Lord

There is one lady
Who comes to our Chapel
Usually on Saturdays
And when she has the time
She loves to spend
Hours and hours
With our Lord
Reading her Bible
Or some holy book
Meditating
Contemplating
Saying her rosary
How she must please
The Heart of God

Her actual name is
Grace Savior
And my thought is
What a Great Grace
The Savior has bestowed on
her
To have this longing and
desire
To spend
All the time she can
With the Lord

What Tremendous Blessings
He must have
In store for her
In this life and in the next!

☙━◆━☙

Helen and Rose
July 4, 2007

Helen and Rose
Are two dear little girls
That come to our Chapel
For Sunday Mass

They are always dressed
So very neat
And so very pretty
And most always
In their beautiful blonde
hair

You will find
A pretty bow or ribbon
To help hold it in place -
perfectly

Helen is 4 ½
And Rose - just turned 3
In May - 2007

I couldn't believe it
But one Sunday
I heard Helen
Reciting the entire Creed
By heart
That's Amazing!

I later discovered
That she had
A little child's Mass Book
So that she could follow along

Their parents
Mr. Dominic Henry
And his very beautiful wife
- Erin
Truly make
A beautiful couple
And it is a wonderful sight
To see them
Shower these dear little girls
With so much love and care

You can see
They are the joy and delight
Of their hearts

May God Forever Bless
And keep them
A Beautiful Family
P.S.
Sometime ago
They moved back home
To Kansas
On Sunday - August 8, 2010
They were passing thru
On their way to Florida
For their summer vacation
So they stopped by

It was so good
To see them
And also to meet
Erin's parents
How!
Helen and Rose had grown!
Helen was 7 now
But would have a birthday
In a few weeks
And would also
Be in 3rd grade this year
Rose is 6
And will be in 1st grade

And to our great delight
We met the new member
Of the Family
Chubby Little James!

◦━━▲━━◦

Mr. Michael Alexander
August 13, 2010

I was standing
In the Sanctuary
Of our Chapel
And I happened to look
Toward the Sacred Heart
Shrine
As I admired
The beautiful bouquet of
Red Roses
Placed there
I thought about
Mr. Michael Alexander
And all the time he spent
Taking pictures
Of the Sacred Heart
From various angles
And with just
The right amount of light
He was very professional

Mr. Alexander
Is the photographer

For the
Georgia Bulletin
And he and a co-worker
Came out
To the Monastery
And really
Spent the day with us
They got an up-close look
Of Monastic Life

Mr. Alexander's co-worker
Would be writing an article
About our
400th Anniversary
Of being founded as a
Religious Order
The Order of the Visitation
of Holy Mary
And
Mr. Alexander
Would be taking
A lot of pictures
Showing glimpses
Of our Life
The article
Came out in the
December 2009 issue
Of the Georgia Bulletin
We thought
They did a wonderful job

This was the first time

That I had met
Mr. Alexander's co-worker
He seemed like
A nice man
But Mr. Alexander
I had known
For quite some time

Over the years
He has covered
Some of the events
At the Monastery

One in particular
That I remember
Was the
Consecration of our New Altar
By Archbishop John Donahue
It was really something to behold
And he was there
With his camera
To capture
Some of it
He really seems to love his job
Another time
Three of us were at
Vocation Day
And at some point

During the day
Mr. Alexander
Came by our Section
Jotted down some information
Took pictures
And soon
There we were
In the Georgia Bulletin

I believe
It was
The last time
That he was here
That he told me
He and his wife
Had celebrated
Their 25th Wedding Anniversary
How Wonderful to hear of this Silver Jubilee

May God continue
To Bless their marriage
And let their love for each other
Ever grow
And maybe
One day
I will come across Mr. Alexander
Taking Pictures

Along
The Beautiful Pathways of
Heaven

Margaret's Translation
August 24, 2010

This morning
As I said the prayer
To Our Lady
Under the title
Of Madonna di Rosa
I thought of
Margaret
She was here for a while
During 2009
On a Vocation Retreat

I somehow
Came to have
A Madonna di Rosa holy card
I believe someone
Sent them to us
Along with a little
information
About Our Lady
Under this particular title
However
It was in Italian!

How glad I was
When I found out
That Margaret
Could translate
The prayer on the holy card
for me
And some of the other
information
About this title
Which I found very
interesting
Originally
Margaret
Comes from the Philippines
But she lived in Italy
For a while
Thereby
Learning the language

For some time now
I have kept this prayer
At my place in the Chapel
For I say it
Almost everyday
I like it very much
And it has become
Quite precious to me
I am very grateful
To Margaret
For this kindness

May God Bless her always
And someday
Bring her to Paradise
And bestow
A special gift upon her
For this
Precious Translation

P.S.
I believe Margaret's last
name is Wong

○━━◆━━○

Mr. and Mrs. Kenneth Brockway
August 27, 2010

Mr. and Mrs. Brockway
Come to our Chapel
Two special times
Each year
Both are to honor
The memory
Of their beloved son
Kenny Brockway
They have a Mass said for him
Each time

August 14th
Was the date of his birth

And November 15th
Is the day
Their dear son
Left this world
At the age of 29

He must have truly been
A wonderful son
For you can see
How much they loved him!
And you can see
How much they miss him!

May God
Be always near
Mr. and Mrs. Brockway
And may He grant them
His Loving Peace

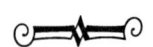

○━━◆━━○

Kenny's Flowers
August 27, 2010

Mrs. Brockway
Always brings
A lovely bouquet of flowers
For these 2 Masses

This year of 2010
On August 14th
She brought

A large vase
Of white daisies
And I believe a type of mum
That was also white

Well!
The white flowers
Lasted and lasted
But every day or so
I would remove a green leather leaf
Until finally
Only the flowers
Were left
It was the day before
The Feast Day of the Apostle
Saint Bartholomew
August 24th
So as
A little special gift to him
And I did not think
That Kenny
Or Mrs. Brockway
Would mind
I took the white flowers
That still looked very good
And I arranged them
In two small vases
And put them on
Each side of the Tabernacle
For the Feast

On Thursday
August 26th
Mrs. Brockway came
To pick up the Liturgy
And it was my time
To answer the door
So I took her
Over to the Chapel
And showed her
Kenny's flowers

She was delighted!

P.S.
They lasted until August 31st
When September
Knocked at the door

⁌——⁍

Mrs. Brockway's Painting
August 28, 2010

One day
A while back
When Mr. Brockway
Came to the Monastery
He brought
A large painting
For us to see

170

And he left it
For several days

I believe
I was coming
From the Refectory
Or from that area
When I came upon it
Near Mother's office
It was stunning!

It was of a woman
Who looked to be
An Indian or a Mexican
The painting was done
In great detail
In a brown pastel color
Her features
Were so impressive

Mrs. Eunice Brockway's
Painting
Is truly
A Most Beautiful Work of
Art!

The Great Surprise!
August 27, 2010

The doorbell rang

And I answered it
Thinking it was our
Confessor
Father Fallon
I was surprised to find
That it was Mr. Brockway
One of our dear
Monastery friends
Who is kind enough
To print
Our weekly liturgy
For the hymns
We sing at Mass
That was
His purpose in coming

After he handed me
The beautifully prepared
liturgy
He said that
He had something for me
To my Great Surprise
He handed me
Some copies
Of the poem I wrote
And often give out
That is entitled
Child of My Heart
It was so beautifully done
And had a most beautiful
picture
Of the Sacred Heart on it

I was speechless!
It was such a
Total Surprise!
And so very unexpected!

I some how
Managed to thank him
But there
Were just no words
To convey
What I felt
May
My Precious Sacred Heart
Take over
And thank him for me
With some very
Special Gift
That will really delight
Mr. Brockway's heart

Emma and Hannah
November 18, 2010

Mr. Brockway
Came to bring the Liturgy
A little after 3 pm
He and Mrs. Brockway
Brought their little grand-
daughter
With them
When they came to Mass
On November 15, 2010
She was ever so cute

Her blonde curls
Bounced all about
As she greeted me
With one of the sweetest
Little smiles
And she was just
As happy as she could be
And quite well-behaved
She is two years old now
And a great delight
To her grand-parents
Mr. and Mrs. Brockway

When Mr. Brockway came
I opened the door
And showed him to the
parlor
I asked him
How was his little grand-
daughter
And of course
A big smile
Came upon his face
And as he spoke
I knew
That Emma Grace
Was blessed

With wonderful and very
loving
Grand-parents

P.S.
They now have
A new grand baby
To shower
With that special love
Emma Grace
Has a little baby sister
Named - Hannah Elizabeth

May God watch over them
Always

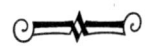

⚜

Dr. Charles R. Stearns

Dr. Stearns
We have heard
That you and your wife
Are going to be
Honorary Co-Chairmen
For the
Relay For Life Walk
To be held in Lilburn,
Georgia
On April 25, 2008
A benefit to help
The American Cancer

Society
A most worthy Cause

As cloistered Religious
Of the
Order of the Visitation of
Holy Mary
We cannot leave our
Monastery
To come out
And join in the festivities
But we will cheer you on
From afar
And send up a few extra
prayers
To give you a boost
In the race

This is so little
Compared
To all you have done for us

I myself
Sister Mary of the Sacred
Heart
Met you
Over 17 years ago
Shortly after I entered
The Monastery in Snellville
A tooth decided to flare up
Right at Thanksgiving time
You were called

And it was taken care of
Right away

Since then
You have had me come in
Every six months
For check-ups
And you have come to know
How I feel about
That Dental Chair!
Most of my life
It has been
Outright Fright!

In my later years
I have gotten
Somewhat calmer
And with your gentle
And expert touch
Along with that smile
And cheer in your voice
And just a super staff
I am at last
A lot better
Even though you tell me
That Dental Chair!
Is going to be
My Purgatory!

Over the years
You have taken
Wonderful Care

Of all of our Sisters
With a heart
Overflowing with generosity
That has no limits
And you have given us
Not only wonderful care
But you have shown
A True Concern for us
And most of all
You have shown
A special love for each of us
That just shines forth
When we're in your presence

And we want you to know
That you are
Ever So Dear
To our hearts
And we are ever so grateful
For all you have done for us

Dr. Stearns
For all your goodness
And Kindness
And overflowing generosity
of heart
For us
And so many
That have crossed your path
I believe
When you cross over
The sea of life

And touch the eternal shores
Of the Beautiful Land of
Paradise
You will find yourself
Within
A Golden Realm
Filled with so many
Precious and rare gifts
That it will take you
Almost forever
To see them all
For the Great God
Our Dear Heavenly Father
Will not fail
To show you
The Depths of His Love
His Goodness and Kindness
And a Generosity
That is lost
In Infinity

Dr. Laurence Lesser
September 15, 2010

Dr. Laurence Lesser
Is a most wonderful doctor
Here in Snellville

Some time ago
I was engaging in an activity
That I had not done in years
I began to have
Some chest pain
And thought
I had better
Have it checked out
As it happened
One of the Sisters
Had cancelled her
appointment
With Dr. Lesser
So I was able to go
In her place
He ran some tests
And they came out okay
Except it was found
That I had
High Cholesterol
So I was given something
That has done well
In keeping it under control

When I went in for a check-up
Dr. Lesser
Greeted me warmly
And during
The course of the
appointment
He told me
How much he really
admired

Our vocation and dedication
He spoke with a deep
respect
For our way of life

God gives everyone
A certain vocation in life
And perhaps
Dr. Lesser has not reflected
Too much on the Fact
Of his own special vocation
That of being
A Wonderful Doctor

How many many lives
Have he helped to save
How many have received
Extra years of life
Because of his excellent care
Extra years
That some may have needed
To get things
Right with God
How many has he helped
With soft words of
consolation
I am sure
In all his years of practice
It is countless

So Dr. Lesser
I want to say

Thank You
For saying yes
To your vocation
And Thank You
For your real care and
concern
For your patients
May God Forever Bless You

Saint Thomas Aquinas Church Group
November 14, 2010

On Friday Afternoon
November 12, 2010
Around 1:00 p.m.
A group of around 18
people
Came on Pilgrimage
To our Monastery
They wanted to spend
Some time
In order to gain
The plenary indulgence
That was extended to us by
the Holy Father
Pope Benedict XVI
For this year long
celebration
Of our being Founded

400 years
As a Religious Order

They prayed very quietly
For a while
And I was told
At some point
They were going
To say the Rosary
After that
Mother would give them
A little talk

When Mother finished
speaking to them
They came back to the
Chapel
To listen to us
Chant
The Office of Daytime
Prayer
When it was over
Mother asked me
To open the Chapel gate
So they could go out directly
From the Chapel
However
By the time I got the key
And reached them
Most had gone back up the
hallway
And left thru the front door

Except for a few
And with these few
I had a most
Delightful little chat
As we made our way
To the front door
And then paused
For a few minutes
On the porch entrance
I learned
They were a group of friends
Who try to do
Good things together
Such as
Coming here on Pilgrimage
And the like

It was really wonderful
To meet
A group of people
Trying to live
A deeper spiritual life
In today's world

We spoke
A few more minutes
And then
They departed

May God continue
To bless their group

And may
The Sacred Heart
Bestow
An extra special blessing
Upon those I spoke with
Mary
Rosemary
A gentleman named Chris
And there was another lady
Whose name
I can't remember
But I do recall
That she had
A very lovely smile

Kathy Gestar
November 16, 2010
I met
Kathy Gestar
In Kroger one day
When I was buying flowers
She thought
That she had taken
Something that I wanted
I told her
No!
She had not!

We then chatted
For a few minutes

And she told me
That she has seen
The other Sisters
At Kroger sometimes

She went on
To ask me about
The dogs - Peter and Paul
She said
When she passes by
For she lives in our area
She keeps trying to see them

We really had
A nice little chat
Then we said Goodbye
And went our way

But I hope
And pray
That God will always
Bless and take care of
Kathy Gestar

Charles and Dorothy Revard
November 20, 2010

Mr. Charles Revard

And his wife, Dorothy
Came to our Monastery today
On this Feast
Of the Presentation of Our Lady
In the Temple
I did not see them
Because
It was not time for me
To answer the door
But after dinner
When I came out of the
    Refectory
I saw our large cart
Loaded down
With all kinds of things
They had brought us
It was quite a variety
Including
I am happy to say
A number of cookie mixes
To help our
Sweet Tooth

Every now and then
They pay us
A surprise visit
Like this
And we are
So very grateful to them
For their kindness

They no longer work
But have retired
And thought
The Economy is not good
At this time
They so willingly and lovingly
Share with us
What they have

How Beautiful this must be
In God's eyes

May God Bless them always
And when they reach
Their Eternal destiny
May He be waiting
To share with them
An Abundance
Of His Eternal Riches

⁕

Sister Elizabeth's Sweet Kindness
December 11, 2010

The Sacristy
Was very busy
The week of December 5th - 12th, 2010

Because we had
Three very special days
Close together
The Immaculate Conception
- December 8th
Our Lady of Guadalupe
Celebrated on December
11th this year
And then
Rose Sunday would be
December 12th
Therefore
We were very busy with
preparations

One night
I was going
To stay up late
After Night Prayer
To finish
Any ironing
That had to be done
And to make a special
bouquet
To put in front of the Altar
For Rose Sunday
To my surprise
Sister Elizabeth
Our new Novice
Showed up
She had gotten permission
From our Superior

To stay up and help me
I had already finished the
ironing
And I would have to work
alone
On the flowers
But I was so grateful
For her thoughtfulness

I thanked her
And may God bless her
Ever so much
For her
Sweet Kindness

Mr. and Mrs. Minder
December 27, 2010

I thought of the Minders
today
When I happened to look
up
And see a little box
That I received
A gift in last month
I thought of all the boxes
The jars and different
containers
That the Minders
Would fill for us

With candy and cookies
Each year for Christmas

They were always
Wrapped beautifully
And it looked as though
They had spent
A lot of time
Doing it
And doing it so lovingly
And it seemed to me
With a lot of Joy

I really
Looked forward
To this special gift
Every year

May God Bless
Mr. and Mrs. Minder
For all the Joy
They gave us
At Christmas
And may they someday
Be rewarded
With A
Spectacular Christmas
In Heaven

In the Year of 2011

Tino
February 2, 2011

Tino
Is a nice young man
That has come
To our Chapel
For a number of years
Usually
On First Friday
For the 7:30 pm Mass
That is in honor
Of the Sacred Heart
Occasionally
He may come
To one of our other Masses

Whenever
He notices
That I may need
A little help
He gets right up

And offers
To assist me
Several times
He has helped me
To carry hymn books
And put them away
I really appreciate it

And once
Sometime ago
I asked him
To help Father
As an altar server
And he gladly did so

A day
When he came for Mass
I happened to be outside
Sweeping the side walk
While it was still cool
He immediately came over
And asked to help
I was nearly through
But I was thankful
That he finished up for me
He then told me
If I ever need any help
Just let him know

I remembered
A little later
That it was time to change

All the missalettes
That we use for Mass
So I took him up on his
offer right away
And he stayed after Mass
And changed them
Earlier
While we were outside
Tino told me
That due to schedule
changes
He could not always come
here
When he would like
He is a Nurse
And works at the VA

But
As I showed him
Where to put the old
missalettes
How happy I was
To hear him say
That he was able to get off
To attend
His parents' 50th Wedding
Anniversary
In the Philippines
Around a year or so ago
That was really
Something very special
And I want to say

Congratulations
To Mr. and Mrs. Lorzano
May they be a light to others
To hold firm
To their marriage
commitment
And may God Grant them
many wonderful Blessings

He also told me
That his parents
Had been to our Chapel
When they came
On a visit here
To see him
And he believed
It was Mother Jozefa
Kowalewski
Who had given them
The statue of an Angel
Which they greatly treasure

The bell sounded
And I had to go to Prayer
So I thanked Tino
And I pray
That the Sacred Heart
Will graciously bless him
much
And always keep him
Close to His Heart

P.S.
Tino's full name is Faustina
Lorzano
I didn't know that for a long
time and
besides that - I understood
him to say
Dino instead of Tino. I do
have it
straight at last

Ana Maria Vidarte
March 6, 2011

Ana Maria
Is from Columbia
She loves
To come to our Chapel
For Mass
And sometimes
Whenever she can
She will make
A Special Visit
During the day
To spend
Time in prayer
She is really very devout

When I was on Retreat
Last October - 2010

She came for 8:30 a.m. Mass
And then stayed on
Almost 'til noon

Her working hours
Have now changed
So she cannot come
As often as she used to
But when she does come
If I happen to see her
And be nearby
She gives me
A big hug
And that beautiful smile of hers
Lights up her face
Like brilliant sunshine

May God bless her always
And may the Sacred Heart
Who she loves dearly
Always keep her
And her dear husband
In His Special care

P.S.
She introduced me to her husband
On one occasion
He seems to be
Quite a nice young man
I pray that God
Will bless
Their marriage
Forever

―――※―――

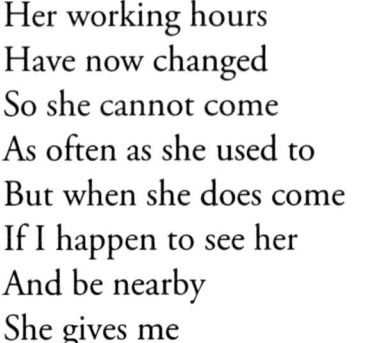

Sandra Znosko
May 25, 2011

What a wonderful surprise
It was
To see
Sandra Znosko
Standing there
When I opened the front door

I had not seen her
In a while
For she had been working
Out of town
For a time

She is now back home
And working
In a hospital
In a nearby town

She is a Nurse
And really loves it
For many years
She worked with children

And they have
A most special place
In her heart
Now she works
With many different cases
And I am sure
She gives them
Her loving care and
attention

I remember
When she told me
About a time
When she stopped to help
With an Accident
On the highway
I am sure
All those involved
Were very grateful
For her assistance

At some point
As she spoke today
She told me
Of the Beautiful Moment
With her Father
He had been very ill
And she was hoping
To be with him
During his last moments
Upon this earth
God granted her

This special favor
And she was
So very grateful
As I listened
The love for her Father
Overflowed
And I glimpsed
Tears
Filling her eyes

She had come
To arrange a Mass
For someone
Who had died
Another example
Of her loving and caring
For others

Soon after this
She had to go
Because her husband John
Was waiting for her
In the car

They were just coming back
From a trip to
The Blue Ridge Mountains
It was to celebrate
Their 25th Wedding
Anniversary
A little early
Because

She was off from work
The actual date is May 29th, 2011

I told them
That was Wonderful!

I was glad to hear
About their Silver Jubilee
For it is wonderful
When couples stay Faithful
To their
Marriage Commitment

I pray that God
Will truly bless
Sandra and John
And fill
The rest of their lives
With peace, joy, and happiness

The Special Offer
June 8, 2011

When they were
About to depart
Sandra said
If there was anything
That she could do for us
To please let her know
And her husband John
Also said
That he could do most anything
And would be glad
To help us too
I thanked them
And how I pray
That God will bless them
In a very special way
For their kindness and generosity
In this Special Offer

Bear
May 31, 2011

After Sandra Znosko
Arranged the Mass
She told me
She wanted me to see
Bear! The Family Dog

So we headed
Towards the front entrance
When we got there
I stayed on the porch
While she walked
A short distance
And called to her husband

To bring Bear

Well!
Her husband did not
understand
That she wanted him
To drive up in the car
So he just opened the door
And!
Bear leaped out!
Running towards us
In happy glee

I was hoping
That he would pause
And stay by her
But!
He was too excited
Because
He saw a new person
That he wanted to meet -
Me!
He was still running
As I heard Sandra say
He's going to jump

I thought
I better get back inside
Before he reaches me
For Bear
Was not a little dog
So I quickly

Went in
And closed the door
A few moments later
I opened the door a little
And he was all ready
To come into the Monastery
To have
An adventurous time!

I needed
To get something for Sandra
And this seemed to be
The perfect time
To go and get it

A few minutes later
I returned
And I saw
That Bear
Was back in the car

Sandra
Was waiting for me
Next to the car
So I went down the walk
And was more formally
Introduced
To Bear
He really is beautiful
With his long golden hair
Very friendly
And bursting with energy

Like a pup
Though he is over a year old

I gave him a pat
Then said
A few words of Goodbye
To all
And moments later
Sandra and her husband
John
And Bear!
Sped away!

The Little Memento

Before Sandra
Got in the car to leave
She gave me something
That she had been holding
Close to her

Something
That was so very special
To her and her husband

Something
That filled their lives
With much joy and
happiness

This something
Was a picture
Of their two daughters
Arika and Lindsey
Whose beauty
Like their Mother's
Is truly
Something!
To behold!

Mr. Angelo Bione
May 31, 2011

I had
Some of Mr. Bione's
Grilled bar-b-que chicken
I have not had any
In years
It was
So very very good!

It made me think
Of the times
When my Father
Would bar-be-que
He really was
A good cook too

I then remembered
How we would

Load up the car
With goodies
For the 4th of July Holiday
And go to the park for hours
And have
A Wonderful Picnic
Which included
Daddy's bar-b-que chicken
Oh! How we enjoyed it!

Now!
Back to the present!
Sometimes Mr. Bione
Includes his string beans
He has a special recipe
Maybe a secret one - I am not sure
But!
Whatever the recipe is
They are
The Best String Beans
I have ever tasted!

We really enjoyed
Our Memorial Day dinner
And we are so grateful
To Mr. and Mrs. Bione

May God reward them
Abundantly
In this life
And

May He one day
Sit them down
At His table
To enjoy a dinner
Beyond anything they can imagine
In the golden glow of
Paradise

⚜

Mrs. Debbie Bione
July 22, 2011

I happened
To go out the Chapel door
One day
I believe
To lock the gate
And there to my surprise
Was Mrs. Bione
She was checking
The Mass schedule

We talked
For a few moments
And then she told me
To tell Mother
That she would be
Bringing our dinner
For the Fourth of July
She and her husband

Are wonderful cooks
And they love to treat us
On special holidays
By bringing our dinner

Whatever it is
I know
It Will Be Good!

May God Bless them always
For their
Great Kindness to us!

―※―

Billy and Yoda
June 13, 2011

The front door bell rang
And I went to answer it
When I opened the door
There stood Billy
The heating and air-
conditioning man
He had come
To check
One of the air-conditioners
In the infirmary area

He had to wait
A few minutes
So we had

A little chat
And it was then
That Billy told me
About his dog
Yoda
An English yellow Lab

Someone at the place
Where he works
Found him
When he was around
5 months old
He was not able
To locate the owner
So Billy took him
And has had him ever since
He will be 5 years old
In a few months
Around November - 2011

Billy said
He did not start out
Trying to name him
After the dog in the movie
Star Wars
But had tried
Several other names
The dog didn't seem
To care or respond
To any of them
Until he said
Somewhat emphatically

Yoda!!!
He perked right up
And that became
His name

Well
Billy had to go after that
And take care of
The air-conditioner problem
But he wished me
A Wonderful Day
And then
We both went our ways

May God Bless Billy
And always help him
Along the Road of Life
And may
He and Yoda
Remain
Lifetime friends

Sister Sponsa Beltran, O.S.F.
June 14, 2011

As I looked thru
St. Oliver's Church Bulletin
For the week of June 12,
2011
I was so happy to see
A picture of Sister Sponsa
And a full-page write-up
Which was actually a letter from her
To
As she says
Her Dear Family and Co-Missionaries

Sister Sponsa
Is a Wonder!
She was a Nurse
And had worked many years
In Africa
At some point
While she was there
She began helping
Disabled children
Who were abandoned
She took them in
Made a real home for them
She fed them
Clothed them
Took care of their
Medical Needs
And then educated them

She taught them to love
And have a deep concern for others
For I remember a time

When she told us
That she was feeding
Many people
Who daily came to their door
I believe it was
Especially during the war

They agreed
To have only one meal a day
So that others
Could have
A meal a day
Most of all
She taught them to pray
More and more
To love Our Lord
and Our Lady
And to have
A very special love
For her Rosary
Which they prayed
Countless times
During 14 years of war

Sister Sponsa
Loved
Her Liberian Family
And her children there
Have won her heart forever
She probably thought
That she would never be
Parted from them

But now in her eighties
After so many years
Of loving service
Sister Sponsa
Had to return home
To the States
Nearly four years ago

In her letter
In the bulletin
She said
That she is well
And that
Teach Peace
I believe it must be
Some organization
Had stepped in
To carry on her work
So she can be at peace
About her children's welfare

May God
Surround Sister Sponsa
With His loving care
And kindness
All the days
Of the Rest of her life
And when it comes time
For her to leave this world
May He welcome her

Into
The Golden Land of
Paradise
Where she will find
Treasure after Treasure
For all her goodness
And kindness
While she lived
Upon the earth
And may God grant her
The special favor
Of welcoming
Her children
As they come thru
The Golden Gates

Mrs. Edith Locsin
June 15, 2011

I thought about
Mrs. Locsin today
I have not seen her
In some time
I wondered
How she was

Every now and then
She comes to Mass
At our Chapel

Sometimes
She arranges
To have Masses said
For different intentions
When she does
Occasionally it happens
That we get a chance
To have
A nice little chat

Around
A year or so ago
She went
On a Pilgrimage trip
To a number of places in
Italy
To my great delight
On her return
She brought me
Some medals and holy cards
From the places
That she visited
I think my favorite
Is the medal
Of St. Michael the
Archangel
That came from his shrine
Located in a cave
That I believe
Is near the place
Where Padre Pio lived
It is ever so beautiful!

I am very grateful
To Mrs. Locsin
For all of these
Precious Little Treasures

May God grant her
A special reward
For this kind
Thoughtfulness of me
And may He some day
Grant her
The Heights of Heaven

⚜

Alejandro Henao
July 10, 2011

Alejandro
Is a very nice young man
From Columbia
Every now and then
He comes to the Monastery
To pick up hosts
For one of the Churches

When you open the door
He greets you
With a big smile
Which comes
Right thru the phone
If you happen

To be the one
To answer it
When he calls beforehand
To place the order

Sometimes
He and his wife
Come to Mass here
It is always a pleasure
To see them

They now have
A new member
In the family
Little Samuel
Who is the joy
Of their hearts

May God always bless
Alejandro and his family
And keep them safe
During their earthly
pilgrimage

⚜

Alejandro's Wife
June 10, 2011

Today
Alejandro's wife
Came to pick up Hosts

For one of the Parishes
I was on my way
To answer the door
But someone else
Arrived first
However
On my way back
Down the hall
As I passed a window
I happened to see her
And to my surprise
There beside her
Was
Little Samuel!

No longer
A Babe in Arms
But standing and walking about
Here and there
So I turned around
And went back
To greet them
For I had not seen them
In quite some time

She said
They had been doing okay
And were hoping
To get a chance
To come here again
For Mass sometime

Since Little Samuel
Was older

He is now
Two years old
And really cute
I can remember
When she and her husband
Alejandro
Carried him in their arms
And brought him to see us
They had been wanting a child
For some time
And they were just
Filled with joy
As they introduced us
To their little son

We talked
Another few minutes
Then she told Little Samuel
To wave goodbye
But he did not want to
I told her
That was all right
He was just two
So he had the right
To do like
A two-year old

Shortly after this

I said good-bye
For the sun
Was really shining down
Upon my head
I do like it hot
But it was just
A little too much
Even for me!

May God Bless
Maria
And her husband Alejandro
And their son
Little Samuel
Forever!

Mrs. Dorothy Baumgartner
July 22, 2011

I thought of Mrs.
Baumgartner today
When I happened
To look up and see
A very beautiful picture
Of Our Lady of Guadalupe
That she wanted us to have
It is on the wall
By Mother's office
And can be seen

By all
As we pass to and fro
Down the hall

It was very kind
And thoughtful of her
To give this to us
And we are
Ever so grateful
And will always treasure
This special remembrance of her

May God
Forever enfold
Our Dear Mrs. Baumgartner
In His Most Precious Love

Andrew to the Rescue
July 25, 2011

Recently
We got a new
Lectionary Book for Mass
When we tried it
On the podium
In the Sanctuary
It did not fit properly
And kept sliding down
It was a little too long

Mother had
A couple of ideas
And then decided
To call
Our Dear Friend Andrew
Who is an electrician
To see
If he could help
To solve the problem

He came
As soon as he could
And began
To investigate the problem
After hearing Mother's ideas

As I went about
Doing my duties
Which caused me
To go back and forth
In the Chapel
I noticed his deep
concentration
As he considered
What could be done

Mother hoped
That the podium light
Could be moved back
It was possible
But there was

Some problem
If that was done
After
His careful consideration
Of the situation
Andrew
Solved the problem
And was able
To move the light back
And!
To our delight!
The Lectionary Book
Fit perfectly!

Thanks Andrew!
For coming to the Rescue!

May God Bless You -
Greatly!

○═══◆═══○

Mr. Frank Gabriel
August 10, 2011

Mr. Gabriel
Came yesterday
To work
On our water system
In some areas
The cold water faucets
Were not giving out cold

water
But Hot!

Today
To my surprise
As I was doing my laundry
in the basement
In came Mr. Gabriel
And striding along beside him
Were Peter and Paul
They were quite happy
To have a man around
Instead of all these Sisters
They know
He loves dogs
And I believe he has 3

Not too long ago
When something else
Had to be fixed
It required
Mr. Gabriel
And his good Assistant Henry
To dig a deep hole
Within the area that is fenced off
For Peter and Paul

How they watched
Mr. Gabriel and Henry
That day!
And for some days afterwards
They thought
It was a good idea
To dig a few more holes
Here and there!
My! My!

After a while
Mr. Gabriel
Got everything
Working fine
As usual
He is a very good plumber
And
He and Henry
Make a Great Team

May God
Bless both of them
And their families
And may He someday
Bring them to Heaven
To live with Him
Eternally

Mother Jane Francis And Her Guardian Angel
August 16, 2011

Mother Jane Francis
And her Guardian Angel
Have a very special
Relationship

Oftentimes
You will hear her say
I told my Guardian Angel
To do such and such a thing
Or to help her
In some particular situation
In particular
I remember last year
When Father Butler came
To give us a Conference
Around ten o'clock or so
Before his arrival
Mother was helping with dinner preparations
Trying to make sure
That everything
Would be ready by noon
Because after the Conference
Mother was going to give
Father his dinner

Well!
Things went
A little awry
And Mother needed
Some time
To get things
Straightened out
So she informed
Her Guardian Angel
About it
And asked him
To do something!

Believe me!
Something was done!
When Father Butler
Got ready to come
There was some mix-up
About the car or keys
Therefore
It caused him
To be somewhat delayed
He didn't know it
But Mother's Guardian Angel
I am sure had a hand
In this delay
For she had
The exact time
That she needed

Perhaps it would be wise
To get to know
Your Guardian Angel Better

P.S.:
Eve of Our Lady's Birthday
September 7, 2013

Father Butler
Usually comes down
I believe from Massachusetts
At least once a year
So that the Chaplain
At the Cancer Home
Can go on vacation
We always enjoy his visits

I must take a moment here
To extend our very deep gratitude
To all the Sisters
At the Cancer Home
We are just ever so grateful
For all their kindness
And generosity
And all the love
That they have shown us
For so many many years

May God Forever Bless
The Hawthorne Dominican Sisters
Who lovingly serve Him
At the Cancer Home

❦

I would also like to extend
Great Thanks
To the Monks
At the Holy Spirit
Monastery
In Conyers
Who were such a help to the Sisters
When they first came to
Georiga
And since I have been here
From time to time
They lovingly come
And say Mass for us
When needed
They and the Hawthorne Sisters
Have really been
True Friends

When Abbot Bernard was
still here
He would come and see us
On the Feast of St. Nicholas
December 6
And he would bring us
A nice Christmas gift

We always enjoyed his visit
And his red suspenders
With the face of Santa Claus
All over them
Surely got smiles and some
comments

May God forever Bless
These wonderful Monks
Of The Holy Spirit
Monastery
And someday bring them
And the Hawthorne
Dominican Sisters
Into the Light of His
Kingdom

Marien
February 27, 2011

When I answered the phone
Marien's cheery voice
Came ringing thru
She was calling
To speak to Mother
But Mother
Was not available at the time
I believe she said
She would call later
But

Before she hung up
We spoke
A few minutes

She told me about
A new Religious
Community
That had just started
In her area
She seemed
Very pleased about it
And I do hope and pray
They will be successful
If it be God's Will

She then went on
And gave me
A little update
On the children
Most important to her
Is for them
To stay
Close to God
And try to do
What He wills
On the earth
I am sure
This beautiful desire

Of her heart
Is very pleasing to God
I truly pray

That He will grant it
We spoke a few moments
more
And then hung up
But what a pleasant
Little conversation
We had
On this bright sunny day

May God bless
All of them abundantly
And lead them onward
To His Heavenly Land

P.S.
Happy Birthday Marien!

David
August 2011

David
Is Mother Jane Francis' son
And Marien
Happens to be
His very lovely wife

They have 4 beautiful
children
Three girls and one son
Madeleine

Teresa
Mary Patricia
And Robert

When they come
For a visit
We all gather
In the Parlor
And they give us
A little performance
Like Aileen and her family
It is really
A special delight!

They are wonderful singers
And I believe
That Marien and the
children
Even make public
appearances
Occasionally

As we listen to them
Every now and then
I could hear David
Singing along
But mostly
He smiles
Sits back
And admires
The beautiful family
God has given him

I am sure
He is very proud of them
May God continue
To bless each one of them
And always
Hold them in His Loving
Hands

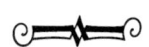

Madeleine's Trip

The last time
They were here
Madeleine
Told us about
Her trip to Australia
To attend
The World Youth Day

It was interesting!
What a privilege
To see
The Holy Father
Pope Benedict
And to be
With so many
Young People
From around the world!

I am sure
It will always be

A treasure
Of her memory

Lora
August 25, 2011

Lora
Is Mother Jane Francis'
daughter
She and her husband - Jim
Came for a visit
From North Carolina
During the Christmas
Holidays

They spent a few days here
But I did not see them
Until the morning
They came to say
Good-bye to Mother
Because they planned on
Leaving town
Around 10 a.m.

I asked Mother
If I could give Lora
The poem card
With
Child of My Heart
Written on it

It is a poem
Which honors
the Sacred Heart
Mother said - Yes

I went to get it
Then I took it
To the parlor
And it was then
That I saw Lora
For the first time
On this visit

I gave her the card
And we talked
For a few minutes
She told me
The Sacred Heart
Was also very special to her
I was quite happy to hear this
For I want
As many people as possible
To come to know and love
The Sacred Heart

Lora
Also spoke of
How she loves
Being a nurse
And working with Hospice
She said

It was truly
A privilege and an honor
I told her
That was Beautiful

As I listened to her
I could see
She really has a love
And true concern
For her patients
May God bless her Forever
For this special
loving care
That she gives to others
And for all her good deeds

And I pray too
That God will someday
Bring her
And her husband, Jim
Into His Heavenly Kingdom

⚜

Mary Rose, Bernadette, Isabell and Mr. and Mrs. Hannish
March 12, 2011

Today
I saw
A beautiful picture

Of Mary Rose
Bernadette
And Isabell
They are really
Beautiful Girls

The picture was taken
In Washington, D.C.
Where they were
participating
In the Walk for Life
What a noble thing
For them to do
To show their support
For Life
What a noble thing for them
To be a voice
For the voiceless unborn

Thinking back
I can remember
Hearing about
The great joy and happiness
Little Mary Rose
Brought into the home
Of Jim and Aileen Hannish
As the First Child

I also remembered
When Bernadette
Was a tiny babe
And the many physical

problems
She had to endure
Before she could leave
The hospital
Her parents
Jim and Aileen
Had to be instructed
I was told
For around 2 weeks
On how to take care
Of all her special needs
But she was welcomed
With open arms
And much love
As time passed
She greatly improved
And a few years later
Little Isabell
Came along
As a dainty
Little bundle of Joy

God
Has really blessed
Mary Rose
Bernadette
And Isabell
With wonderful parents
Who love them
Ever so much
And are
Ever so willing

To do
All they can for them
Today
Mary Rose is 14 years old
Bernadette is 13
And Isabell is 8

They are involved
In all kinds of activities
And sports
Play several musical
instruments
And when
They came on a visit her
Little Isabell
Gave us a performance
On her big cello
We were amazed!

Mary Rose
Bernadette
And Isabell
All have something special
In common
They were all adopted
By Jim and Aileen Hannish

They were given
The Gift of Life
And what
Beautiful Girls
They have become!

Aileen's Beautiful Gift
August 15, 2011

Some years ago
When Aileen was here
On a visit
As I was walking on the hall
I heard the sound
Of her beautiful voice
Singing
The Ave Maria

It is a rare privilege indeed
For us to hear
A professional opera singer!

May she always praise
Glorify
And thank God
For this beautiful gift
That He has bestowed on
her

Shantel
August 27, 2011

One day
When I stopped by

Mother's Office
My eyes fell upon
A picture
That was on her desk
She handed it to me
And told me
It was Shantel
Who was looking
Just as cute
As she could be
And with a smile
That was as bright
As the light of the sun

She is the precious daughter
Of James and Tammy
Williams
The joy and delight
Of their hearts

James
Mother Jane Francis'
youngest son
Is a Musician
And I think
Shantel
Has been trying to play
something
And performing
Since she was
Just a Babe

I remember hearing
Daddy got her some
instrument
That she thoroughly enjoyed
And I am sure
He enjoyed watching her
Enjoy it

Once
When Shantel
Was not feeling so well
I am told
She decided
To have
A little talk with God
Afterwards
She was okay

Shantel
Is about 7 years old now
May she grow up to be
All that God desires
And may she forever be
The light and joy
Of her parents' heart

May God always
Bless their Family

The Little Blue Pumps
September 14, 2011

Yesterday
I stopped by
Star Shoes
I had a squeak
In my shoes
That I could not get out

When I walked in
I was greeted by Don
And soon after
By Janice - his wife
I had not seen them
In a long time

I proceeded
To tell them
About the problem
With my shoes
Don took them
To the back
And Janice and I
Had a nice little chat
At some point
Greg
Who works for them
Joined in
And I was happy

That I got a chance
To see him too

Soon
Don came back
And was ready
For me to try my shoes
As he slipped them
On my feet
He told me
The wonderful story
Of how
He came to Atlanta
And how
He got his job
Working with shoes
I found
His job interview
Was quite interesting

I then got up
And walked around
Inside and outside
And I heard
No Squeak!
Thank Goodness!

In his kindness
Don
Then took my shoes
And minutes later brought
them back

With a beautiful shine
I was most grateful

Before I left
He showed me pictures
Of a lovely pair
Of blue pumps
He told me
They were
The First pair of shoes
That he had made
I was really surprised
Because I didn't know
That he actually made shoes

He and Janice
Now have their own shoe store
I pray
That God will always bless
Don and Janice and Greg
And let them always keep
That beautiful Faith and
Trust in Him
That came thru
As they spoke to me
In our delightful conversation
On this bright and sunny day
In September - 2011

Mr. and Mrs. Charles Matthews
September 17, 2011

Mr. and Mrs. Matthews
Is a wonderful couple
Who come to our Chapel
Very often for weekday Mass
They are quite devout
And love to come
A half-hour early
So they can spend some time
In silent prayer

Recently
I arranged a Mass
For Mr. Matthews
He was hoping
That a certain date in September
Was available
I was able
To give him that date
And I was so glad
That I could do so
Because he told me
That he and Mrs. Matthews
Would be celebrating
Their 55th Wedding

Anniversary
How awesome!
And what an example
Of
Love and Fidelity

As Father
Offers the Mass for them
I will pray that God
Will continue
To bless their
Precious marriage
And keep them safe
Until they reach
Paradise

P.S.
I also want to thank
Mr. and Mrs. Matthews
For all their loving kindness
And generosity to us
And I pray
That God will reward them
From His Great Abundance

September 17, 2011

Around 2 years ago
The floor in the Chapel
Had to be re-done

So the parlor
Was turned into
A little Chapel
For about two months

We put
A small altar in it
With a nice
Little Altar cloth
A small tabernacle
Was placed there
With 2 tall and slim
Flower stands
Folding chairs
Were placed all about
And the sisters' side of the parlor
Was also
Re-arranged
When everything was finished
It did look very nice

As Sacristan
I sat
On the people's side
So that I could
Answer the front door
When the bell rang
To come in for Mass
And also
To take care of

Lighting the candles
And taking out the books
That Father needed
For Mass

One day
It happened
That Mr. Matthews
Took a seat
Near me
And for the first time
I could hear him
Singing
He really does have
A very nice voice

Apparently
He has been keeping this
A little hidden secret
So Mr. Matthews
You will now
Have to sing out
In full voice
And!
Praise the Lord!

Birthdays and Mrs. Norma Matthews
September 17, 2011

Birthdays! Birthdays!
How we love them!
The gifts
The cards
The call
The special words of
remembrance
The party celebration
And of course
How we love that
Birthday Cake!

Some years ago
Our Dear
Mrs. Norma Matthews
Started surprising us
With very delicious
Homemade
Birthday Cakes
Apparently
She somehow
Got a list of our birthdays
So as each one came up
You would hear
The doorbell ring
And when it was answered
There stood
Mrs. Matthews
With a Birthday Cake!

We are ever so grateful
To Mrs. Matthews

211

For this loving kindness to
us

I pray
That when she gets to
Heaven
Our Dear Lord
Will give her
A Grand Party
With a
Birthday Cake
Beyond her dreams

―※―

Mr. Richard Hitchcock
September 17, 2011

Many years ago
Mr. and Mr. Hitchcock
Came to
The Way of the Cross
Services
During Lent

It happened
That Father
Needed someone
To carry the cross
Before him
As he went
From station to station

Mr. Hitchcock
Who is not Catholic
Lovingly carried out
This little service
To help Father
And did so
Very reverently

I believe Our Lord
Was quite pleased
With this
Special little service
That was done for Him

May Our Dear Lord
Grant Mr. Hitchcock
Some special reward
For his kindness
And may He someday
Bring him
And his dear wife
Into
Heaven's Realm

P.S.
Every now and then
We get a nice card
From Mrs. Gloria Hitchcock
We are very grateful
For the kindness to us
And we always remember

her
And Mr. Hitchcock and
their family
In our prayers

May God Bless them always

Mr. Cannon
September 19, 2011

I had not seen
Mr. Cannon
In some time
But when
The Lenten Services began
He came
To the Way of the Cross
That we have
On each Friday of Lent
And he was pleased
To carry
The Processional Cross
For Father this year

Mr. Cannon
Belongs to
The Third Order of
Carmelites
A Religious Group of People
Who seek

A deeper relationship with
God
And strive to walk
Closer in His Way
And according
To His Will

I myself
Belonged to
The Third Order of
Carmelites
In Baton Rouge, Louisiana
Before I entered
Religious Life in 1990
And became
A cloistered contemplative
Nun

I loved it
And all of those
Wonderful People
Forever remain
So dear to my heart

Years ago
I remember
Whenever
Mr. Cannon had an
opportunity
He would come
An hour early for Mass
So that

He could spend the time
In deep meditation
It was most edifying to my
heart

I pray
That God will always keep
Mr. Cannon
Close to Him
And I pray
That
The Sacred Heart
Who Mr. Cannon loves so
dearly
Will surround him
With His Love
On this earth
And then
May He surround him
forever
With His Love
In Heaven

Lady From Maine
September 19, 2011

Mrs. Simonne Faucher
Was on vacation
Here in Georgia
Visiting her daughter

She enjoyed
Staying a while
After Mass
And several times
We spoke a few minutes
When she returned home
To Maine
She sent me
A lovely picture
And told me
About her
80th Birthday Party
I saw
Many beautiful flowers
In the picture
And it looked to be
A Most Wonderful Event
I was glad
That she was able
To celebrate
This Special Birthday

This was quite
Some years ago
But I pray
That she is enwrapped
In the Love of God
Whether
She is on this earth
Or whether
She has departed it

For the realms beyond

P.S.
On the envelope
That she sent to me
She addressed me as
Reverend Sister Mary of the
Sacred Heart
I had not seen
Nor had I ever been
addressed
As - Reverend Sister

Mrs. Hubner
September 19, 2011

During
My first few years
Of Religious Life
There was a lady
Who used to come some time
For Mass

I did not know her well
But there is
One beautiful thing
That I remember about her
She loved to send us
A card

For any holiday
Or special occasion
That came up in the year

They were really
Beautiful cards
And we enjoyed them
Very much
Some time
We kept them displayed
On the shelf
In our Community Room
Like special little treasures

Mrs. Hubner
Departed this earth
Some years ago
I pray
That she found
A Golden Card of Welcome
Awaiting her
When she touched
The Eternal Shores

Mary Ann Kelly
September 19, 2011

Mary Ann Kelly
Often comes to our Chapel
For Mass

One morning
She brought
Her holy water bottle along
And she asked
If I could fill it
I told her - Yes
When I took it back
Into the Sacristy
I noticed
Just how beautiful it was

Etched
Into the bottle itself
Was a picture
Of Our Lady of Lourdes
And kneeling before her
Was St. Bernadette

The bottle was a cloudy white
And looked to be made of
Some type of thick plastic
The Cathedral is on it
And mountains can be seen
In the background
It really is
A very unique looking bottle

When I returned
I asked her
If she had been to Lourdes

She said - No

I pray
That God will someday
Bless Ms. Kelly
With a trip there
If it be His Will
So that she can see
In reality
What she has beheld
In her hands
So long

⚜

The Sweet Gift
September 20, 2011

Last year
About a week before
Christmas
Mary Ann Kelly
Thought of us
As she made
Her Christmas Preparations

To our great delight
She brought us - A Sweet Gift
Two large pans
Of Home-made Cookies

She had made
Quite a variety
There were chocolate chip
cookies,
Pumpkin cookies,
Some kind that had dates
And then some
Special Christmas cookies
They were really
Very good

May God bless her
For her
Sweet kindness
To us
And always keep her
In His loving care

Shoo-Fly Pie
September 20, 2011

I remember
When I was in school
Sometimes
In stories
They would speak of
Shoo-fly pie
I wondered
Just what kind of pie
It was

For I had never seen
Or tasted any
Once I finished school
I don't remember
Ever thinking about it again

Last year- 2010
To my delight
Ms. Mary Ann Kelly
Brought us
Two Shoo-fly pies
From her trip
To the Dutch Country
In Pennsylvania

At last! At last!
I got a chance
To see and taste
Shoo-fly pie
I found it
Very delicious

Thank You! Thank You!
Ms. Mary Ann Kelly
For bringing
This childhood wonderment
Into A reality

A-Roo-Ka and Her Children
September 21, 2011
Sometime ago
There was a lady
Who loved to come
On Sunday afternoon
To spend some time
Before the Blessed
Sacrament
Which was exposed
On the altar
For silent prayer
Before Benediction

Sometimes
She brought her 3 children
Who were very well-
mannered
And they too
Would sit quietly
And pray

I have not seen them
In quite sometime
But I hope and pray
They are well
And may Our Dear Lord
Always bless and keep them
In His very special care

P.S.
I am writing
This dear lady's name
As it sounds

May she pardon me
For not having
A correct spelling

Deacon Evelio Garcia Carreras
September 23, 2011
Deacon Evelio
Came for Benediction
On August 1st
2010
The First Sunday of the
month
Deacon Mobley
Was not able to come
So he asked
Deacon Evelio
To fill in for him

It is always nice
To see
Deacon Evelio

And he likes to come
Whenever
He has an opportunity

Sometimes
His wife Rosa
Comes along
And it is nice
To see her too
Our Dear Sister Caritas
Was her Aunt
And she would come
To visit her
Whenever she could

In May of last year
2010
Deacon Evelio and Rosa
Took a wonderful trip to Italy
He told me
They rented a car
And went - Everywhere

I believe
They stayed a while
In Rome
Then at some point
They drove to Assisi
And the place
Where Padre Pio lived
And a great highlight of this trip
Was seeing
The Holy Shroud
That was exposed
While they were there
They also went
To Florence, Pompeii
And just all about
They had 25 days
And really had
A wonderful time

I was very glad for them
And enjoyed
Listening to their travels
What a special favor of God!

The bell rang
And it was time
For the Deacon
To begin our Evening Services
Which include
Exposition of the Blessed Sacrament,
A half-hour of silent prayer,
The Office of Evening Prayer,
And then closing
With Benediction

We were very grateful

That Deacon Evelio
Could come for Benediction
Which he always does
So devoutly

May God bless him
And his wife Rosa
And someday bring them
To Paradise

Family Tradition
September 23, 2011

I remember
Some years ago
Deacon Evelio's grand-
daughter
Mary Elizabeth
Made her
First Communion
In our Chapel
And not too long ago
His grand-daughter
Katherine
Made her First Communion
In our Chapel also

It is always
A blessing and a joy to us
When we have

Special occasions
And it is wonderful to see
The joy and happiness
Of all the Family that attend.

Mary Elizabeth and
Katherine
Are sisters
And they live in Chicago
Making their First
Communion here
Is more than a special occasion
It is something
Extra Special
Because
This is where
Their Mother
Made her First
Communion!

P.S.
They have a brother
Around 4 years old
And sweet little Cecilia
Who is
Ever so cute
Is about two

We look forward to seeing
If they will keep up

This Family Tradition

September 26, 2011

I remember
When Deacon Evelio
Served the Mass
For Father Sunny
I was very much edified
With all the love
Care and reverence
He showed
In purifying
The chalice and the paten

The love
He has for Our Lord
Came shining thru
May He always bless him
With this special love
And reverence of Him

September 25, 2011

As I looked out
The Refectory window
This morning
I gazed upon

The statue of Our Lady
Holding the Child Jesus
Upon her arm

I remembered
How hard
Our dear friend
Kris Klein
Had worked
2 or 3 summers ago
Planting flowers
All about and around Our Lady
When they came out
Our Lady had
A beautiful flower garden

There were all kinds
And so many different colors
And I took great delight
In the beautiful morning glories
That climbed the tree behind it
For they are one
Of my favorite flowers

I believe
When our dear Kris
Reaches Paradise
She will find
That Our Lady

And the Sweet Child Jesus
Have planted her
A flower garden
With beauty
No human words
Could ever describe

St. Joseph's Feast Day
March 19, 2013

P.S. I also want to thank
Our dear Kris
For all the very generous help
That she gave me
In the Sacristy

And for all her
Sweet kindness
In remembering each one of us
On our birthdays
With a card
And some little
Special gift
May God always bless
And take special care
Of Kris Klein
A very dear and gentle
Sweet lady

In the Year of 2012

Mr. and Mrs. Kevin Doyle
November 27, 2012

Mr. and Mrs. Kevin Doyle
Are a very dear couple
That have come to our chapel
For many years
They have been very kind
And generous to us
And we are most grateful

Sometimes
On special occasions
Such as Mother's Day
Or Father's Day
Or on their birthday
The whole family comes
To honor
And show their love
For them

Children and grandchildren
They are a lovely sight to
behold
And you can see
The happiness
Upon their faces

Sunday after Sunday
You can see the love
This couple has
For each other
Shining thru ever so brightly

A number of years ago
Mrs. Doyle
Had a stroke
And I am told
It was to the quick action
Of Mr. Doyle
That she swiftly arrived
At the hospital

This happened
Before I came
To know them
But what I have observed
Week end and out
Is the loving attention
Mr. Doyle
Bestows on his wife
She does very well
But sometimes

She needs a little help
To get about
And he is always there
At her side
With loving assistance

They are always
Full of smiles
And Mrs. Doyle
Told me that Mr. Doyle
Is always
Full of Jokes

I am glad
That God has blessed them
With a
Wonderful Marriage
And I pray
That He will someday bless
them
With Wonderful Treasures
In His
Garden of Paradise

Mrs. Doyle's Precious Revelation
November 25, 2012

One day Mrs. Doyle
Asked me

To write down the names
Of all the Sisters
She then proceeded to tell me
That when she wakes up
During the night - around 3 a.m.
She prays for each Sister

How loving and kind of her
It really touched my heart

And it brings to mind
The Fact
That we do not know
How often
We have been helped
By the prayers of others

Let us take some time now
To thank God
For all those
Who have helped us
And let us ask him
To bless
And take care of them
Always
And someday
Bring them to His Kingdom

I also ask
My Dear Sacred Heart

To forever enfold
Mrs. Diane Doyle in His arms
For her sweet preciousness
To us

Thank You Mrs. Doyle
Ever so much!

Mr. Doyle's Two Beautiful Gestures
November 27, 2012

Mr. Doyle
Came to know
Father Hogan well
While he was a Chaplain
At our Monastery
Some years ago

Father Hogan
Is now retired
But Mr. Doyle
Sees him from time to time

Whenever
The Missalettes are changed out
In the Chapel
And new ones put in

Mr. Doyle knows that I have
An extra one or two
Large print missals available
So he always remembers
To ask me
For one
For his friend

P.S.
When I was
In the Novitiate
Mr. Doyle
Thought I had
A special need
And extended to me
His gracious kindness
It had been taken care of
But I want to thank him now
For his beautiful and kind gesture
To me

May God Always Bless Mr. Doyle!

Mr. Doyle's Grandsons
November 27, 2012
I had not seen
Mr. Doyle's grandsons
In a while
When I happened
To see them in the Chapel
recently
I thought
My Goodness!
How they have grown!
They are almost
All Grown-up!

I remember
When they were young
They would come and assist
Father
At the
Way of the Cross
During Lent

Other times
They and Mr. Doyle
Would come and assist
At Special Occasions
Throughout the year

Mr. Doyle
Would wear an alb
And the boys would wear
Altar server's attire
They would all look so nice
And really make
These occasions
Ever more special

I want to thank them now
For their kind service
And I pray
That God will reward
Mr. Doyle
And his dear grandsons
Generously in this life
And much more generously
In the next

Dr. and Mrs. Stephen Brena
December 9, 2012

Dr. and Mrs. Brena
Is a very lovely couple
Who come
To our Monastery

They bring us wonderful treats
From time to time
And we know
They love us dearly
But they do have
A very special reason
For coming
To our Monastery
And that is

To see their daughter -
Sister Margaret Mary

When she comes
Into their presence
You can see their faces
Light up
With overflowing love
And they are
So Happy
That she is a Religious
Serving God
In the Special Call
That He has given her

Then
Looking upon
Sister Margaret Mary's face
You will see her glowing
And bubbling over
With love
For her dear parents

It is
A most beautiful picture

May God
Forever capture
This picture
And keep it so
Until
He can capture

An even more beautiful one
Of all of them
In His Heavenly Kingdom

Dr. Brena's Touching Concern
November 27, 2012

Whenever
Dr. Brena
Came to Mass
He would ask me
How my Sister Roberta was
For she was very ill
At the time

After some months
She departed this world
In January of 1998

Then
Whenever Dr. Brena
Came to Mass
He would tell me
I am praying
For your sister - Roberta

Later
He did the same
With my Mother

And when she left this world
He told me
He was praying for her too

My heart
Was truly touched
And I was most grateful
For Dr. Brena's
Loving concern

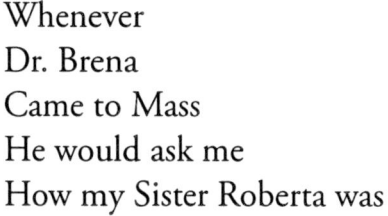

Mrs. Brena's Gracious Help
November 27, 2012

Christmas
And
New Year's Day
We have
Midnight Mass
At the Monastery
And the hour before
We have
A Holy Hour
Which includes
The Divine Office
The public
Is welcome to attend

Since
Sister Margaret Mary and I

Have to be at
The Divine Office
Mrs. Brena
Likes to come
And help us out
By passing out
The programs
For the Divine Office
And for Mass
As the people come in

She has been very faithful
In doing this
Over the years
And Sister Margaret Mary
and I
Have been very grateful
For her kind help
Which she carries out
So graciously
In our Sacristy charge

May God grant
Dear Mrs. Bianco Brena
A very special reward

The Birthday Cake
November 28, 2012

Every year

In July
We looked forward
To a very special treat
Sister Margaret Mary's
Birthday Cake

Dr. and Mrs. Brena
Would order it
From the bakery
And it never failed
To be delivered on time

It was always
Beautifully decorated
And always
So very delicious

What made it special
Was under the icing
Half of the cake was white
And the other half was
chocolate
So the Sisters
That could not eat chocolate
Could have a piece
Of the other side

How thoughtful and
considerate
Of Dr. and Mrs. Brena

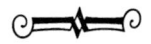

Mr. and Mrs. Raymond Holstein
December 9, 2012

Mr. and Mrs. Holstein
Is a very sweet couple
That use to attend Mass
often
At our Monastery
I have not seen them
In quite some time
Because
They are now
In their golden years
And cannot get about
Like they use too

But I remember
The time
When they came to
celebrate
Their 50th Wedding
Anniversary
What a special day!
They looked so nice
And so did their family
Who also attended
The Special Mass

Afterwards

They went to the parlor
To find
A special breakfast
Prepared for them

I remember
They were very happy
That day
I pray that God
Will always let them hold
The joy and happiness
Of that beautiful day
In their hearts

The Sweetest Card
November 27, 2012

Sometime ago
I had a number of
Child of My Heart poems
Printed up
To give out
During
The Feast of the Sacred
Heart
And other
Appropriate times
I was very grateful to
Mother
For this favor

She knows
How I love the Sacred Heart
And want to bring others to
Him

I believe
It was at Christmas Time
That I still had some left
So I asked Mother
If I could send one to
Mr. and Mrs. Holstein
She said okay
And soon after
I put it in the mail

A short time later
I received
The sweetest card
From them
They were so very glad
That I had sent them one
And have now put it
In a very special place

I was very touched
And how I pray
That God will forever bless
Mr. and Mrs. Holstein
One of the sweetest couples
I have met
On my Journey thru life

Jim and Justine
December 17, 2012

Jim and Justine
Are a newlywed couple
That visit our chapel
sometime
They live in Florida
But wanted to be married
In this area
Where some family
members live

They both were previously
married
For many years
Until the day
Their spouses
Entered
Eternity

Now
In their golden years
They were blessed by God
To find each other
And
Fall in love
The Feast of the Visitation
Is special to them
And they chose it

As their
Wedding Day!

How wonderful!
It must have truly
Touched the hearts
Of Our Lord and Our Lady

After the Wedding
They came
To make a visit in our
Chapel
And
The beautiful bride
Left her bouquet
It was placed in the
Sanctuary
By Our Lady
And!
It lasted and lasted and lasted!

I pray that God will forever
Let them hold
The happiness of that day
In their hearts

In the Year of 2013

Mr. and Mrs. Michael Bruyere
January 17, 2013

Mr. and Mrs. Bruyere
Are a lovely couple
Who come to our Chapel
From time to time
For the 7:30 p.m. Mass
On First Fridays

Sometimes
They bring along
The whole family
Their daughters
Rebecca and Sarah
And when Mrs. Bruyere's
Mother
Is visiting from Alabama
She comes along too
I am always delighted to see her

She is such
A lovely lady

During
The Christmas Holidays
I was pleasantly surprised
When they gave me
A little gift
It was a book
Entitled - Treasury of
Novenas
It contains
Many beautiful prayers
And it has become
Ever so precious
To my heart

I am very grateful
For their thoughtfulness
And kindness
I pray
That the Sacred Heart
Will always
Keep a careful watch
Over their family
And bestow upon them
Many Blessings

Mrs. Veronica Bruyere
January 18, 2013

Sometimes
Mrs. Bruyere
Attends
Our Week day Masses
And when she has time
She likes to spend
Some time afterwards
In quiet prayer

She has a deep love
And concern
For her family
Wanting
Just the best for them

As I have come to know her
I have found
That she tries to keep God
In all her decisions
And prays for his Guidance
And help in her Life
She knows His Will
Is always - The Best

I pray that God will always
Keep her close to Him
As she journeys thru this life

And may He forever
Keep her close to Him
In Paradise

The Wedding Pictures
December 15, 2010

Mrs. Bruyere's daughter
Rebecca
Is a newly-wed
And in December - 2010
Mrs. Bruyere
Brought the pictures
For me to see
And they were left overnight
So that I could share them
With the Community
At Recreation
I really enjoyed
Looking at them
They were so very beautiful

There was a picture
Of Mr. Bruyere and Rebecca
Coming up the aisle
Going toward the altar
I am sure
When he looks back at it
It will always be
Special to his heart

Mrs. Bruyere
Looked so very lovely
That I believe Mr. Bruyere
Couldn't help
But think
Of their
Wedding Day

There was a beautiful picture
Of the groom
And his side of the family
His Mother and Father -
Mr. and Mrs. McDonald,
His brother and his wife
And their two sons
Who were ever so cute
Also his sister
And her husband
And he was even blessed
To have
His grandmother there
They all came down from
Canada
To share this Happy Day

There was also a picture
Of the bride
Who was ever so beautiful
Standing with her side of the
family
Mr. and Mrs. Bruyere - her

parents,
Her dear grandmother,
Her sister Sarah
And Mrs. Bruyere's brother
Along with his wife and son

Of course
There were beautiful pictures
Of the bride and groom
One particular one
Was outside
At Stone Mountain Park
Where they had their reception
And also taken outside
Was a most stunning
Black and White picture
Of the Newly-Weds
Mr. and Mrs. Ian McDonald

At some point
Amid all the celebration
The bride and groom
Took a break
And another beautiful picture of them
Was captured
As they sat
In the big rocking chairs
On the porch
At Stone Mountain

This beautiful celebration
Did finally come to an end
And the bride and groom
Waved good-bye
As they departed
For their Honeymoon

May God Bless them always
And forever grant them
The Happiness
Of
Their Wedding Day!

⸙

Two Precious Pictures
January 19, 2013

Two more Precious Pictures
Of Ian and Rebecca's
Wedding
Was his grandmother
And Rebecca's grandmother
Walking hand and hand
Down the aisle
Smiling
Filled
With all the happiness
Of this beautiful day

Then the other
Precious Picture

234

That I saw
Was the bride's grandmother
On the dance floor
Dancing with her son

Both of these
Are little treasures
That will forever bring
Warmth to the heart

Sarah's Gift
May 22, 2010

Sarah
This gift
I am giving you
Is a little used
But I don't' think
You will mind
For it is filled
With Spiritual treasure
That will be of help to you
And a source of help
To many others
That you will meet
On the Road of Life

Mother Francis de Sales Cassidy
January 22, 2013

In 1954
Mother Francis de Sales
Cassidy
Brought
The Visitation Order of
Holy Mary
To Atlanta

She had been a member
Of the Toledo, Ohio
Community
And for many years
She dreamed
Of making a Foundation
In her home state of Georgia
Her dream
Finally became a reality
And she and a group of
Sisters
Set out
To make the new
Foundation
In Atlanta

Since then
All thru these many years

Mother Cassidy's Family
Have just been
So wonderful
So kind
And so very generous
To us
And we truly thank them
From our hearts

And now
I would like to lift up a prayer
And ask
The Great King of Heaven
To reward them from His abundant riches
While they journey on earth
And when they depart for Eternity
May He reward them with - Paradise

Gloria Gilbert
January, 2013

Gloria Gilbert
Was a precious little old lady
That use to come
To our Chapel sometimes
On Sunday

She was very tiny and delicate
And when I came to know her
She was nearly 90 years old

I believe
She lived in some place
That had assisted living
Our dear Mr. Houff
Another nice gentleman
That comes to our Chapel
Goes by
And picks her up
And brings her
To Mass with him
How kind of him
And how pleasing
This must be to God

I was always
Glad to see her
And she inspired you
To be attentive to prayer
For whenever
I happened to glance her way
Her head would be
Bowed down in prayer

In 2009
She departed this world

At the age of 92 or 93
And
It was only
After her death
That I found out
That she had once been
Quite famous

Mr. Houff and I
Were speaking about her
one day
And he began telling me
About her life
And he even brought
Some news articles one day
To share with us

Gloria
Was from Boston
And danced in the fifties
Her real name
Was Marjorie
But her agent said
It was too long
Her Mother
Saw something passing by
With the name Gloria on it
And said
Call her that
They lived on Gilbert Street
And now Marjorie
Became Gloria Gilbert

Gloria
Went on to appear
On the Ed Sullivan T.V.
show
The Milton Berle Show
She danced on Broadway
And I believe
She was at
The Radio City Music Hall
She also appeared with
Betty Davis
Eddie Cantor
The Andrews Sisters
And in Chicago
Her name
Was up in lights

During her career
She preformed
In a number of European
Countries
London
Paris
And a little article showed
That she would be at
The Follies de Paris Revue
From December 26th -
January 9th
No year was shown
She even performed - down
under

237

In Australia

Along with the news articles
Mr. Houff
Included a picture of her
Standing
On her toes
She was truly beautiful
When she was young
And for a time
She held a record
Of being
The only one in the world
Who could turn around
Three-hundred times
We believe - in around 3 minutes
Or thereabouts

I tell you
I was quite surprised!
I never would have dreamed
That this
Tiny little old lady
Had been such a celebrity

Without saying a word
Gloria
This precious little old lady
Has taught us much
About
The virtue of Humility

P.S.
Thank you Mr. Houff
For sharing this with me
And our community
May God bless and reward you
For all the kindness
That you showed
To Gloria Gilbert
And for the kindness
Of sharing her life
With us

⚜

A Nice Gift
January 21, 2013
Mr. Houff
Is a man
Very mild in manner
Who tries to walk closely
In the path of God

One day
He spoke to me
About having
A Mass said
For his dear Mother -
Monica Houff
Who had departed this earth
And touched Eternity

He wanted me
To arrange it
Around Mother's Day
If it was possible
I believe it was
And I thought
What a nice gift
For a son
To give his Mother

May God bless Mr. Houff
For his loving
thoughtfulness

Faithful
January 23, 2013

Gloria
For many many years
Was truly Faithful
In coming
To the Monastery
For the monthly
Guard of Honor meeting
Which honors
The Sacred Heart of Jesus
Who is very dear to her

After the meeting
She loved to stay on

For awhile
And spend some quiet time
Before the Blessed
Sacrament
And then
She would join us
For the
Office of Evening Prayer
And Benediction

From time to time
She would come
And make a retreat with us
And there was a hope
That she might have
A vocation
To our Order

This hope however
Had to be put aside
For a few years ago
Gloria
Gave us her happy news
Of being
A new bride
Gloria Anionwu
Had become
Gloria Chukwuma
God had truly blessed her
By giving her a spouse
From her own Country
Of Africa

She brought
A Wedding picture
For us to see
And of course
The bride and groom
Were all aglow with
happiness

Since then
A few years have passed
And she could not
Always come to the monthly
meeting
Because
She and her dear husband
Have been blessed
With a cute
Little son and daughter
And taking care of these 2
tots
Really fills her days

Not too long ago
Gloria gave me
A beautiful picture
Of her family
It will always be
One of my little treasures
And I pray
That God will always
Help and protect

Their Family
And fill their lives
With many blessings
Especially
The Blessing of Paradise

The Little Visit
January 26, 2013

Gloria
Came to our Chapel today
I had not seen her
In a very long time
She looked good
As she always did
And as usual
Her hair was arranged
In one of her
Many different styles
That was always
So very becoming

We got a chance
To have
A real nice little visit
And she caught me up
On the happenings in her
life
Since I last saw her

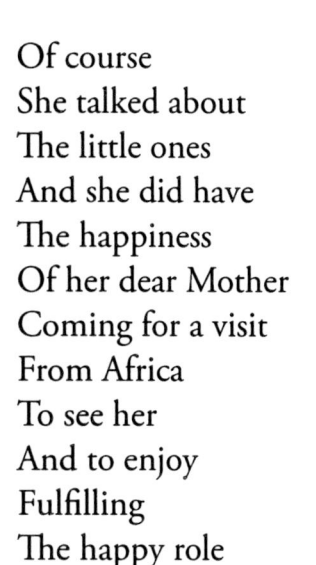

Of course
She talked about
The little ones
And she did have
The happiness
Of her dear Mother
Coming for a visit
From Africa
To see her
And to enjoy
Fulfilling
The happy role
Of Grandmother

Gloria
Had also experienced
Some sadness
In the loss
Of her older sister
But God
Was helping her
To cope with it
And I know
The Sacred Heart
Whom she loves dearly
Would always stay near
We talked about
A number of things
During this little visit
Then Gloria said goodbye
And departed

A Special Custom
January 27, 2013

When
Our dear Gloria
Was awaiting her first child
She told us
That in her Country
The husband
Chooses the name
Of the child

She went on
To tell us
Some of the names
Her husband
Was pondering over
She did not know
At that time
What he would
Decide upon

In our American culture
It is not that way
But thinking on it
I thought
What a special responsibility
That has been given
To the Father-to-be

Mr. Coppinger
January 24, 2013

Mr. Coppinger
Is a real handyman
Who gives us
A helping hand sometime
At the Monastery

I myself
Was in some need
For I had just recently
Moved to another room

Well! I was going thru
Something!
That I had never
experienced!
At night I felt like
I was going
To be dumped out
Of my bed!

I came to discover
That the foot of the bed
Was higher
Than the head of the bed
And I felt
I would be dumped right out
At the head of the bed
I then
Tried to see
If I could get the bed
adjusted
I got - no where!
I then asked
One of My dear Sisters
To help me
And we got - nowhere!
I thought
Something!
Will have to be done
About this situation
Because I can't keep
Trying!
To sleep like this!

So Mother
Let Mr. Coppinger
Come in
And check out the problem
At first
He got - no where!
But - at last
Thanks be to God
He found the problem
And was then
Able to get my bed
Adjusted!
Hallelujah!

P.S.
Thank you! Thank you!
Mr. Coppinger
May God grant you
A million blessings
And someday bring
You and your very lovely wife
Home to Heaven
Where Everything Works Right!
And where
You will be able
To rest
Eternally!

Mrs. Hamilton and Tom
January 27, 2013

Mrs. Hamilton
And her son Tom
Have been dear friends
Of our Monastery
For quite a number of years

They love to surprise us
With a special gift
Often times

Our friends will bring us
Gifts that are real treats
That we might not have otherwise
Expensive candies
Gourmet foods
Special coffees
And so forth
For which
We are most grateful
And really enjoy on Feast days
But Mrs. Hamilton and Tom
From time to time
Like to bring us
The gift of some groceries
Of practical - everyday things

Milk
Eggs
Regular Coffee
Can Goods
Paper Goods
Just those things
That are needed everyday
We really appreciate them
And they can be
Marked off
The grocery list

Whenever they hear
That the weather
Is going to be bad
They give us a call
To make sure
That we have
Everything we need
And sometimes
They just go ahead
And bring us something
Just in case
There is some snow and ice
And we are unable to get out
How very thoughtful of them

Afterwards
They like to make
A little visit
To our Chapel
For a few minutes

Mrs. Hamilton and Tom
Take a real joy
In giving to us
This most precious gift
May God reward them abundantly
For their thoughtfulness and kindness

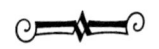

The Birthday Bouquet
February 20, 2013

Mrs. Hamilton called
She wanted
To bring us a gift
She had received some flowers
For her birthday
And
She wanted
To give them to us

They were really beautiful
And I placed them
In the Sanctuary

I know
It must have pleased God
That she wanted
To share her bouquet
With Him

I pray
That when she reaches
Heaven
She will be greeted
With a
Heavenly Bouquet
Filled with flowers

Unknown to earth

Mr. Mackin
January 31, 2013

For a number of years
Mr. Mackin
Came to Mass
At our Chapel
From time to time
During his latter years
He was really an inspiration
For he suffered with his back
And had other physical problems
But he didn't let them
Keep him down
He kept going
And came to Mass
As often as he could

I remember one day
When I answered
The front door
There he was
With medical equipment in-hand
Bringing us
A special gift of his kindness

I really thanked him
For caring so much for us
That he would
Go out of his way
To make this special trip
When he was not well

I remember another day
When he spoke of
Accepting his sufferings
As The Will of God for him
He offered them up
And seemed to have
A serene peace

Mr. Mackin's sufferings
Ended
On Christmas Eve
December 24, 2009
When he departed this earth
To enter
Eternity
What a day to leave this world!
And
What a Christmas
Celebration!

A Beautiful Gift
January 31, 2013

Soon after
Mr. Mackin's departure
His long-time friends
Came together
And decided
To do something
Really special for him
and something
That I am sure
Touched
The heart of his dear wife
Mrs. Mackin
They arranged
To have a Mass said for him
On the twenty-fourth day
Of each month
For a year

I thought
What a beautiful gift!

⚜

The Nerone's and Their Friends
January 31, 2013

Mr. and Mrs. Nerone
Attended Mass
At our Chapel sometimes
And besides on Sunday

I remember
They liked to come on
Wednesday
Because their schedules
Allowed them to come
together
On that day

They are very nice
And I remember a time
When Mrs. Nerone brought
us
Some special bread
That she had baked
I doubt
If there was a crumb left!

I came to know
Some of their friends
When they attended the
Mass
On the 24th of each month
For their dear friend
Mr. Mackin

It happened one day
When I went out
To close the Chapel gate
Quite some time after Mass
I saw
That some of the people
Were still out front

When they saw me
They greeted me
And introduced themselves
We spoke a few minutes
And that is when they
informed me
That they had been friends
For 30 years or more
They did not move away
After finishing school
But stayed right here in the
area
They became very close
Over the years
And had watched
Each other's children
Grow Up

I knew
Mrs. Mackin
For I had met her
Sometime ago
When she came to Mass
With her dear husband
She was always very nice
And really had
A very lovely smile

I also
Already knew
Mr. and Mrs. Nerone
For they had been coming

To our Chapel awhile

But I did not know
The Kennedys
The Proctors
And The Stricklands
Until just recently

They really seemed
To enjoy each other
And I am sure
They have been
A loving comfort
To Mrs. Mackin

It was wonderful
To meet
A group of people
Who have been
Close Friends
For so many years
Because
In today's world
People frequently move
From one place to another
And most times
Lose touch with friends

I pray that God will bless
The Nerones and their
friends
And always keep them close

To each other
And may He someday
Let them share
Eternity
In His Paradise

Mrs. Maureen Casey
February 9, 2013

Mrs. Maureen Casey
Is another lovely lady
Who often comes
To our Chapel

Over time
I came to know her
And one day
She told me
That she had participated
Many years ago
In a
Walk for Peace
I believe
That it started
In Washington State
And went across the Nation
To the East Coast
From there
They crossed the sea
And at some point

Reached Ireland
The Walk
Would continue from there
Until they reached
The Holy Land

I believe
Mrs. Casey told me
That she joined The Walk
When it reached Virginia
And I believe
It was sometime after
They reached Ireland
That she had to depart
She was a Nurse
And her daughter
Was in a very serious
accident
So she came back
To take care of her
When
The Walk for Peace
Was nearly at an end
Her daughter was better
And God blessed her
For she was able
To rejoin The Walk
And take
The Final Few Steps

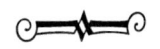

248

The Parting Picture
February 9, 2013

When
Mrs. Maureen Casey
Found out
That I was going on leave
To discern further
If God was calling me
To start
A new Religious Order or
Congregation
In the Church
She left the Chapel
Shortly after Mass
But soon returned
With a very special gift for me

It was wrapped nicely
In red and white
When I opened it
It was a very beautiful picture
Of the Sacred Heart
From days gone by

She told me
That it was
A part of her home
But somehow
It seemed

That I should have it
So she very lovingly
Gave it to me
I was so very touched
And will forever treasure
This most precious gift

―――

Gloria Still
February 15, 2013

Sometimes
I go to Still Lake Florist and Nursery
To get flowers for the Chapel
For Feast Days and Holy Days

Gloria
The owner
Is very nice
And meets you
With a warm smile

She is very helpful
And so are the people
Who work for her
Sometimes
I have a hard time
Deciding on bows
And what color of paper to

use
If I am getting some potted plants
To help in our Christmas decorations
The lady
That usually helps me with this
Is very kind and patient
I believe her name is Carol
I really appreciate her help
And lovely decorations

However
Most times
I am the one
Who will be
Making the flower arrangements
So I go here and there
Because Gloria has a large selection
Choosing the different flowers
To make the bouquets
That not only go in the Chapel
And then down the hallways
And a few other places
Where we have a statue
To honor Our Lady or St. Joseph
And sometimes
They are placed for the Superior
On her special days

So it is quite a blessing
That when all the flowers
Are totaled at the register
Gloria
Gives us
A nice discount

We are
So very grateful to her
For her kindness and generosity to us
May God bless her abundantly
And some day surround her
In His Heavenly Kingdom
With the beauty of flowers
She has never seen

☙━◆━❧

Still Lake
February 16, 2013

On my trips
To Still Lake Florist and Nursery
In Lawrenceville

I had always noticed
The small body of water
Near it

I never thought
Much about it
Nor had I considered
That it had a name
But one day
I happened to find out
That Gloria's last name
Is - Still
And apparently
That body of water
Is on her property
Hence - the name
Still Lake Florist and
Nursery

What a surprise to me!

⸻

The Special Arrangement
February 16, 2013

When
My Dear Aunt Martha died
I was given permission
To go to Still Lake Florist
And send a flower
arrangement
For the funeral

I wanted it
To be very beautiful
Because my Aunt
Was so very dear
To my heart

Gloria contacted
The Winnsboro Flower
Shop
In Winnsboro, LA
She proceeded to tell them
That we wanted
A very special
Pink and white bouquet
made
For someone very special
And she then
Went on to tell
The person that answered
A little about Aunt Martha

I was very grateful to Gloria
For I was so very pleased
To find out
That the Winnsboro Flower
Shop
Had truly made
A most beautiful pink and
white bouquet

For My Dear Aunt Martha

May God Bless
Gloria Still
And may God Bless
The Winnsboro Flower
Shop

───※───

Dr. Richard Carlin
February 18, 2013

Dr. Richard Carlin
Is a very wonderful
Eye doctor
And has seen our Sisters
For many years

He is always
So very nice
And so are the people
Who work in his office

I remember a time
When I was seeing
Another doctor in his office
That particular day
And Dr. Carlin
Happened to be passing by
When he saw me
He took a seat beside me

And we had
A nice little chat
It had been quite a while
Since I had seen him
So I was glad
That he had a few minutes
To stop by

Again
Sometime passed by
Before it was time
For my check-up
As it happened
It was near
The end of August - 2011
Just a few weeks
Before my 2-year leave
From the Monastery
Was about to begin

Dr. Carlin himself
Was now mainly
Doing eye surgery
And he was growing so
much
That he built
A big new beautiful office
Down the street
From where he was

He did not sell
His office building

But turned his former office
Into his surgical clinic

The day of my appointment
I got a chance to see
The new office
Truly beautiful
And at some point
We met
And had another
Nice little chat

I told him
I would soon be going on leave
To discern further
If God was calling me
To start
A new Religious Order or Congregation
He was very much interested
And really hoped
The best for me

While I was there
He introduced me
To his son and daughter
Who were also
Eye doctors there
How wonderful!
And I know
This must truly

Warm his heart

I want to Thank
Dr. Carlin
For all his goodness and kindness
To me and all the Sisters
All these years
And I pray
That God will continue
To bless him abundantly
In this life
And when he leaves this earth
May he forever enjoy
The Light of Paradise
Which far exceeds any light
The human eye can stand

Part Seven

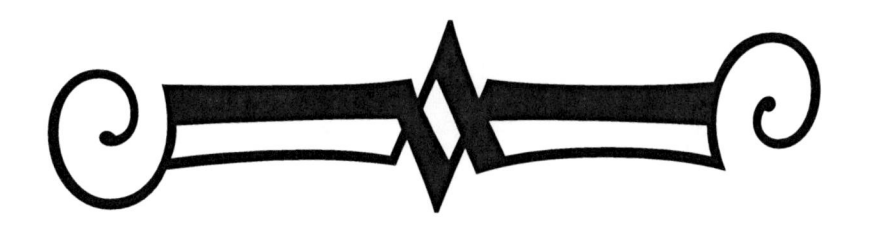

Sister Sunila
and
The Coyotes

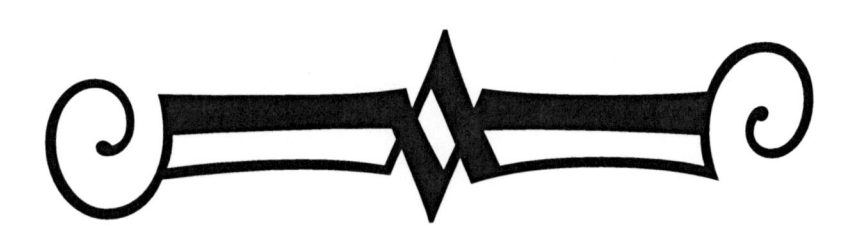

The Coyotes
February 8, 2009

Oh!
The Coyotes! The Coyotes!
Came
And took up residence
On our Monastery Grounds
At Maryfield
To my great dismay

One day
At mealtime
We happened to look out
The Refectory windows
And there
By the pond
We saw 4 coyotes!
My! My!

They were
Filled with energy
And just played about
Here and there
So I concluded
They must be teenagers
At some point
The parents showed up
And after a while
They were gone

Good Riddance!

Well I hoped
That was the end of them
But!
Oh No!
It was not!
That was only
The Beginning

For about
The next nine months
We were plagued
With their presence
They made themselves
Right at home
Upon our 26 acres
Which included
A little bridge
Across the pond
And two little wooded areas
And also
Next to us
Is another large tract of land
Where they could go
For more fun and adventure

I tell you!
There were
No more leisurely walks
And sitting out
In the warm sunshine

At reading time
For Me!

Before I went outside
To get in the car
I would look
Carefully around
Then make
A quick dash
And hop in!
When I reached the gate
I would hop out quickly
Unlock it
Drive through
Then rush out again
To relock it
Then back to the vehicle
Breathing
A sigh of relief
For once
In the distance
I had seen one
Looking toward the gate

One morning during Mass
They made an awful noise
And Father mentioned
To the people
That the coyotes
Had the Sisters
In somewhat of an upstir

It was reported
To city Authorities
And we called
A number of Agencies
And it seemed
That no help
Could be had
Unless
The coyote had rabies

We did hear
Of one being found with it
In a town
That was not far from us
For these coyotes
Were in
A number of towns
Around the Atlanta area

In our plight
We resorted
To having someone come
Who was
A cross-bow hunter
He sat calmly
For hours
The coyotes never showed
up

We had been told
That they are
Quite smart

257

And move about a lot

Well!
There was little more
That we could do
And Finally
After about 9 months
They moved their residence
Elsewhere!
But!
For the next year or so
Every now and then
They would drop in
For an unexpected visit

Well
It's been quite sometime
Since we have seen
Any of them
And last Summer - 2008
I was able
To take leisurely walks
And sit in the warm
sunshine
At Reading time
Without having to keep
A watch out
For
Mr. Coyote

Sister Sunila's Little Adventurous Plight
February 3, 2009

Sister Sunila
Is our Novice
And one day
She had a
Little Adventurous Plight

As she came out
Of the Novitiate Building
And started back
To the Main Building
She happened to look
towards
The beautiful grotto
Of Our Lady of Lourdes
And to her surprise
There she saw
Three Coyotes!

Well!
She lost no time
Though trying to remain
Composed
So that
She would not attract
Their attention
And cause them
To decide
To come her way

For a closer look

Lo and behold!
When she got
To the top of the stairs
And turned
The knob on the door
She found
That it was
Locked!
Oh No!

Well
She went back down the stairs
As the coyotes watched
And tried to stride
Calmly
To the next available door
That was
A little distance away

She soon turned
The corner
And the door
Came in sight
Thank Goodness!
And no coyotes
Seemed to be following her
Perhaps Our Lady
Had them in hand!

At last
She reached the door
Of the well-traveled hallway
And to her shock!
She found it
Locked!
And apparently
No one
On the well-traveled hall
My! My!

Nothing to do now
But go back down
To the sidewalk
That would be
In view
Of the coyotes
And go all the way across
The building
To the basement laundry door

Still trying
To stride calmly
She headed that way
With no coyotes following
Finally!
She saw the laundry door
And to her
Great Relief
It was unlocked!

I am sure
She lifted up
A prayer to God
And a special one
To Our Lady of Lourdes
For keeping her safe
In this
Little Adventurous Plight

Sister Sunila
February 2, 2009

I have spoken
Of Sister Sunila
And her little adventure
With the coyotes
But now
I want to say
A few words
On her kindness and
generosity

During the year
We celebrate
A number of Feastdays
That make the Sacristy
A very busy place
Especially during
The Christmas Holidays

And even more busy
During Holy Week
And
The Great Feast of Easter

At times I am in need
Of extra hands
Especially Christmas and
Holy Week Time
Dear Sister Sunila
Though busy herself
Is ever ready
To put aside
Or put on hold
What she is doing
To lend a hand

And what
I find remarkable
When you ask her
For help
A big smile
Lights up her face
And she says
Yes!
Or
Sure! I would be glad to!
It's a privilege!
And oftentimes
She adds
For the Lord!

Once
When her Mother was
visiting
From New York
We spoke
For a few moments
And I told her
What a help
Sister Sunila was to me
When I needed it
She then told me
That Sister Sunila
Had always been that way
Ever ready to help

With all that she does
I try not to impose on her
But when there is
A real need
I always get
That lovely smile
And that
Overflowing joyful
willingness to help
For which
I am most grateful

May the Sacred Heart
Grant her
Many Special Blessings
For all her kindness
And generosity

And may He someday
Show her
An abundance
Of His Kindness and
Generosity
In the Glory of Paradise

Sogi, Susan, Sharon, Stephanie and Little Serene

Sister Sunila
Has a Sister named Susan
Who lives
In a nearby town
Since I help
With answering the door
Sometimes
I get a chance
To see her
And her family
When they come for a visit

She has a daughter
Named Sharon
Who is 17 years old now
And another one
Named Stephanie
Who will be 16 soon
I tell you

I can hardly tell
The Mother
From the daughters
She looks so young!

And Then!
There is
Sweet Serene
Their little bundle of joy
Who is so dear
To Sister Sunila's heart

As I tell them
How beautiful
They all look
Especially when they wear
Their native dress of India
A warm smile
Filled with love
Lights up the face
Of Susan's husband - Sogi
For he knows
What a Treasure
They are

And I know
That he too
Is the
Very Special Treasure
Of their hearts

February 7, 2010

One time
Quite a few
Family Members
Came to visit Sister Sunila
I believe
It was during Thanksgiving
Time

While they were here
Her brother's son - Nevin
And his daughter - Ellen
Her sister Stella's son - Alvin
And her daughter - Vivian
Along with her sister Susan's
daughters
Sharon and Stephanie
Gave our Community
A little unexpected
performance
They sang for us!
What beautiful voices
They have
What joy filled our being
As we listened to them
Sing the songs of their hearts
Including some
From the Land of India

How they touched us
That Beautiful Day
When the Beautiful Family
Was gathered in our Parlor

⚜

Her Father's Happiness

Sister Sunila
Took her Temporary Vows
Of three years
On the Feast Day of
St. Thomas the Apostle
July 3, 2008
At that time
She received
Her new Religious Name
Sister Theresa Maria

She is from India
And it is believed
That St. Thomas
Brought the Gospel of Good News
To their Land
So it is a day
That is very special
To the people of her Land

Many of her
Beautiful Family
Came for the occasion
For it is a big step
In Religious Life

Retired Archbishop John Donahue
Celebrated the Mass
I was glad to see him
Because it has been
Quite some time
Since he has been
To our Monastery
He looked great!

There were
A number of priests
And deacons
And the ceremony
Went quite well

Afterwards
There was a Reception
For everyone
In the Parlor

It was during this time
That I got a chance
To speak
To her father
And he told me
That he was
So proud of her

As he spoke
I could see
The sparkle of tears
In his eyes
Because
His joy and happiness
Was so Great!

Mrs. Kulangara
February 7, 2010

Mrs. Kulangara
Is a lovely lady
Who has
A deep love and concern
For all her children
Her grandchildren
And for all her family

Whenever possible
She does not fail
To be with them
On important dates
Of their life
Baptisms - Confirmations - and so forth

It is always special to me
When I happen to answer the phone

And she is on the other line
It is a real pleasure
To talk to her
For a few moments
Before I go to get her daughter
One night
I believe it was
After she had spoken to her
Sister Sunila told me
Of the Sweetness
Of Mrs. Kulangara
I could hear
The joy in her voice
And see
The deep love
That she has
For her Mother

Little Serene
February 26, 2009

Little Serene
Is just as cute
As she can be

Her hair is cut short
And it is
So very becoming
It makes her face

Look like
A perfect picture

She is always dressed neat
And I remember
A time that she came
Wearing one of the latest
styles
In tennis shoes
They flashed while she walked
They were something to behold!

Sometimes
When she comes for a visit
To see her
Kunjaunty - Little Aunt
She is all full of energy
Other times
She is in
Daddy's arms
Taking a nap

When she is taken
To the Chapel
She tries hard
To behave well
But occasionally
Her curiosity
Gets the better of her
And she checks out

A few things
Quietly

When it's time to go
I am sure she takes
A last glance
At her Kunjaunty
To receive
A sweet smile of goodbye

⁘———⁘

Little Steven
March 19, 2009

Little Steven
Is the son
Of Sister Sunila's brother
Joseph
He lives in New York

I don't think
I have seen him
More than once
And that was
When he was resting
On his Mother's lap
Surrounded
By her loving arms

He is five
And very cute

I don't know much about
him
But I was told
By Sister Sunila
That when Little Serene
Who is four
Went on a visit to New York
To see the family
Little Steven told her
That he was older
Than her
Therefore
She had to
Respect him!

⚜

The Beautiful Family

Last year
2008
Sister Sunila's Father
Mr. James Kulangara
Turned 70
And there was
A Big Birthday Celebration
For him
In New York
Where he lives

Many Many
Family members gathered

From a number of places
Including India and Canada
Brothers
Sisters
Children
Grandchildren
And so many other
Family Members
All in All
It was some Celebration!

You may wonder
How I know this
Sister Sunila
Is a cloistered contemplative
Religious
Of our Community
And she could not attend
So they sent her
A very special and unique
Photo Album
She shared it with us
And it was
Truly a joy
To look through
All those pictures
And see
The Happiness
Of this Beautiful Family
That really try
To stay together

Part Eight

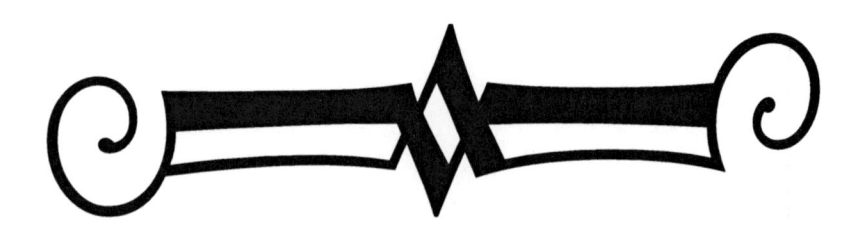

Little Stories
and
Little Little Stories

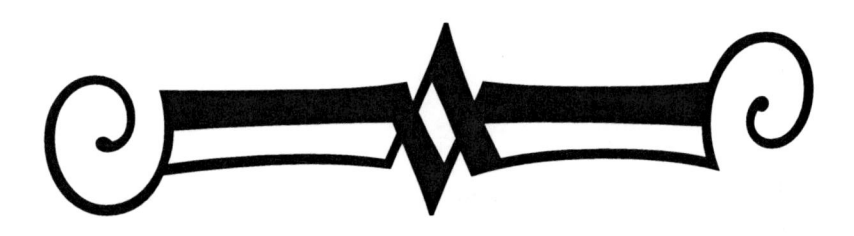

J.J. and The Coyotes
February 8, 2009

J.J.
Is our beautiful
Golden colored
Shaggy dog

The Vet
Gave him to us
Some years ago
After Little Joe died
A sweet
Little black and white dog
That we had for many years

When J.J. first came
To the Monastery
He would not go
Much beyond
The carport area
Apparently
He had been confined
To a certain area
When I noticed this
I felt sorry for him
Because he had
All this land - 26 acres
That he could roam

After some time went by
I happened
To look out of the window
one day
And to my delight
I saw J.J.
Way in the distance
Trotting along
Near the boundary fence of
the property
From then on
He checked out
His Territory
And made his rounds often

For a short time
A very small dog
Somehow managed
To find a way
To gain
Entrance
To our property
J.J. took him for a friend
And they had
A good time together

Then!
Without Warning!
The Coyotes Moved In!
And poor J.J.
Lost His Freedom
For we had

To keep him in the
basement
And when
He was taken outside
He was tied to the carport
With a long rope

This was for his safety
But I was sorry
This had to be

As time went on
If the coyotes
Had not been seen
For a while
Sister
Would allow him to run free
To his happy delight

But one day
It was not
As safe as was thought
And as we looked out
The Refectory window
There sat J.J.
Out on the grounds
Looking toward
The edge of the woods
Where two young coyotes
Were looking toward him
Oh My!

Moments later
When he was called
Instead of coming
Toward the basement
He started running
Toward them
It took him
No time
To cover the distance
And into the woods
They went

From the sounds we heard
Some of us thought
That we had seen
The Last
Of our Dear J.J.
But soon
They emerged from the woods
And!
To our relief!
And surprise!
J.J. had them on the run!

I do not recall
Ever seeing
Those young coyotes again!

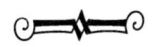

Ring! Ring!
June 10, 2003

Sister Jeanne Marie
Is our dear Portress
And many a mile
She travels a day
From one end of the
Monastery
To the other

Along with this duty
Goes
The Telephone
Which increases
By leaps and bounds
Her mileage a day

Oftentimes
As soon as you hear
Ring! Ring! at the door
And you see her
Promptly start out
You will then hear
A Ring-a-ling-ling
From the phone

She tries to handle both
But
When this is not possible

One of her dear Sisters
Lends her a hand

One day
When she was away for a
while
I was asked
To perform this duty

I believe
It was a Monday morning
But if it was not
It was just like one!
Busy! Busy!
Ring! Ring! At the door
Ring-a-ling-ling! from the
phone
And Then!
Workmen came
To fix the Arm
On the Sacred Heart statute
Out on the grounds
I went from place to place
After being informed
That a certain Sister
Had the Arm in her
possession
Well it seemed like
We were playing
Hide and seek
And the dear Sister was
saying

Find Me If You Can!

By Noon
I was Exhausted!
How happy I was to see
Sister Jeanne Marie
On her Return!

⁂

The Story of Puff
July 2, 2007

Sister Josefa Maria's sister -
Annette
Came today from
Jacksonville, Florida
And will stay for a few days
She brought along her pet
duck
What a surprise to us!

She said one day at work
She saw a baby duck
That was abandoned
Or had been thrown out
As the runt of the litter
Being attacked
By a number of other ducks
She rescued her
And took her home

She then cleaned her up
Fed her
And cared for her
Afterwards
She called several agencies
But could find none to take
her
So she thought
She would get her well
And let her go in about 2
months
At some point she read
That once they are hand-fed
They can no longer exist on
their own
So there she was - With A
Duck!

After about 2 months
She found out
She could get duck diapers
They saved the day!

By this time
She had become quite
attached
To her duck
And had named her Puff

Now Puff
Walks and flies about the
apartment

When Annette is there
And when she goes to work
She is put in a special cage
She gets a tub bath once a week
And with a harness about her
She goes on walks with Annette
Sometimes she gets to ride in the car
And sit about as she likes
She is a joy
To the people who see
This unusual pet
At night
She sleeps so near Annette's head
That when morning comes
Annette finds feathers in her hair

Puff is light gray and white
And makes a most sweet gentle sound
Annette had 2 husky dogs
That had to be put to sleep
She believes
That God sent her Puff
For she has been
A real consolation to her

Puff!
Enjoyed the Sisters
And we enjoyed
Puff!

J. J.
September 24, 2009

When J.J. was young
He used to run
Like the wind
And play about
Everywhere
He was
The King of the Land
All 26 acres
And many a morning
I would see him
In the distance
Patrolling his territory
Near the boundary line

Later in the day
He would be closer
To the Monastery
And that is when
He might
Cause you quite a challenge
As he makes a dash
For the gate

For you would have to
Get out of the van
To open the gate
Drive thru
Then get out
And close the gate

Sometimes
He suddenly
Seemed to appear
From no where
And if he had
The least opportunity
He would
Dash!
Out the Gate
Oh Boy!
Then the chase was on
And you would hear
Come back J.J.
Come back boy!

This happened
But a few times
Then a rope
Was put around
A tree near the gate
So that
If he showed up
You could tie him up
Until you closed the gate

Some years
Have now passed
And we seldom
Have this problem
One day I saw
The reason why
As I looked down
Upon our dear J.J.
I noticed
That his golden coat
Was now
Mingled with gray

The Bird Ordeal
September 22, 2009

One day
When I went out
To take care of
The Chapel gate
I noticed
There was a little bird
In the outside covered area
Where we put
The Nativity Set
At Christmas
The poor little one
Had gotten trapped
In the small opening
Between the bricks

And the plexi-glass
The brick wall
Was only a few feet high
And had the bird persevered
In flying up higher
He could have easily been free
But he just hopped about
Here and there
And would only fly up
About a foot or two
All the while
Becoming
More and more frustrated
And beginning to panic

Well! I didn't know
Quite what to do
So I decided
I would go and get
One of my Sisters
To help me
Sister Mary Peter
Came to my aid

And we tried
One thing and then another
Nothing worked
We eventually
Had to go back in
I was really concerned
About my little feathered friend
But there was nothing more
We could do

The next morning
When I opened the gate
I saw that
My little friend
Was still alive
I was so glad

A Mrs. Niceta Brown
Comes to our Chapel
For Mass sometimes
She came this day
Said a prayer to St. Francis
Then using
The straw part of the broom
Instead of the handle
As we had done
She lowered it
Near the bottom
The bird hopped on
And she
Very slowly and gently
Lifted him out
She saw
That he was in a daze
So she reached out
And took him
In her hands
To soothe and comfort him

Then after a while
She set him free

How I thank God
For Dear Mrs. Niceta Brown
Who saved
The little bird
From his
Great Ordeal

May God bless her always
And may St. Francis
Make her
One of his special friends

The Beauty of the Morn
March 28, 2004

I took a little walk this morning
Along the pathway
All about
Were splashes of violets
Tiny little wildflowers
That blended in
Daffodils
And a number of other flowers

I was hoping to see
Some morning glories
I love them so
But they were not yet in bloom

As I continued on my way
I came upon
J.J.
Our beautiful dog
I told him so
As I reached down
And gave him
A gentle pat
I then went down
Toward the pond
Stood and admired
The pretty picture it made
It has a lovely bridge
That crosses over it
With a little gazebo
In the middle
That has a bench on each side
Where you can sit and read
Think!
Or just enjoy the view

From where I was standing
I looked all around
In the distance I could see
The top of the hermitage

Nearby
I could see
The quaint little well house
Its wood was very dark
But its door
Was very light
A real contrast
There were 2 little evergreen trees
Planted on one side of it
And all about it
There were a number of other trees
Making it look like
A little land of wonder

I heard a small plane overhead
When I looked up
I was lost
In a sea of blue
That was ever so beautiful
And filled with
The light of the sun

After gazing upon all this beauty
I started back
This time
Along a row of tall
Evergreens
As I walked

Taking in the beauty of the grounds
I paused for a few moments
And looked in the distance
At our beautiful
Sacred Heart Shrine

The bell rang
It was time to go in
But how!
I had enjoyed
The Beauty of the Morn

The Best Alarm Clock
May 12, 2011

Well!
I was having
One of those nights!

Twelve o'clock passed
One o'clock passed
And I was
Still awake!

Two o'clock passed
And three o'clock
Came right behind
And I was still awake!
And had had enough!

Of this sleepless night!
So I got up
And took a tablet
That I knew
Would help me sleep

Now!
The rising bell
Would be ringing
In the not-too-distant future
5:30 a.m.
To be exact
And I was afraid
That I might not hear it

So!
No longer having
An alarm clock
I asked
My Guardian Angel Joseph
To wake me up
On time

And of course
As nearly always
He woke me up
Right on time

Thank You!
My dear Sweet Joseph
For you are
The Best Alarm Clock

I could have!

The Flock of Robins
February 28, 2002

When I opened my curtain
This morning
What did I see!
A flock of robins
Enjoying the early morn
They flew all about
From bushes to trees
Pausing but a moment
To perch on the bench
Sometimes on a bush top
Where they would grab off
A little snack
They hopped about the sidewalk
And the ground
And they sang
A very lovely song
While they showed off
Their beautiful rust orange-colored breasts

Eventually
I guess they grew a little tired
Because

When I looked out
The window again - soon
after
They seemed to be resting
But what a special little joy
They had given me
This bright morning

⁂

Thanksgiving Day
November 26, 2009

On this beautiful
Bright and sunny day
I heard
A light plane
Go over
And it made me think about
The time
When I was taking
Flying Lessons
And I was the one
Flying over
On a beautiful, bright, and
sunny day

⁂

Hide and Seek
August 23, 2010

Peter and Paul were playing
As I looked out
Of the Refectory window
After breakfast

I first saw Paul
With his head
Under the trees
Looking like
He was about to pounce
Or attack something

Then I saw Peter
On the other side of the tree
He was acting as though
He was playing
Hide and seek
But soon
He came from behind the
tree
And got after Paul
Paul ran off
And Peter went after him
Then
They began
A little playful tussle
In the yard
After a while
They headed for the
basement
Still playing
A few minutes later

Paul came back outside
And tried to hide
Behind the bush
Near the door
And wait for Peter

Peter
Never came
I think
He decided
That he had had enough
And it was now time
To take a rest

Follow the Leader
August 26, 2010

Looking out
Of the Refectory window
This morning
I saw Peter and Paul playing
Follow the Leader
Wherever Peter went
Paul followed
Walking directly behind him

Along the fence
By the trees
Just wherever
Then they paused

And peeped thru
The tree branches
And soon after
Paul thought
It was time
For another friendly tussle

The tussle turned into
A little friendly wrestling
They both ended up
Stretched out
On the ground
And then decided
To take a little rest

Afterwards
Peter began
To lick Paul's face
And really gave it
A good washing

After
Just a little more
Brotherly play
Paul went off
And Peter's attention
Was diverted
In another direction

But
How plain it is to see
How much these brothers

Love each other

November 4, 2010
As I looked out
The Refectory window
Around dinner time
Peter came out of the basement
And went over
And took one paw
And stepped on Paul
Who was taking a nap
Near the door

Peter woke him up
Tussled with him a little
And then stopped
Though Paul wanted to continue
I guess
Peter just wanted him
Awake!
Because he knew
It was
A little too early
For their rest time

The Little Adventure
September 19, 2011

This evening
As I sat in the Refectory
Just about to eat my dessert
A nice big piece
Of chocolate cake
I was more than surprised
When Peter and Paul
Came rushing in

The cat was being taken down
And somehow
They had a chance
To run up the basement stairs
And then
Come bounding
Into the Refectory

Someone called them
Of course they didn't come
They were on
An Adventure

They ran around
To nearly every Sister's place
Gave a sniff

And went onto the next one
I grabbed my cake
And headed for the kitchen
And before I knew it
They had beat me there
Then they took a little tour
Of the kitchen
Soon after this
They were
Finally apprehended
And guided back
To the basement door
As soon as
They started down the stairs
The door was closed swiftly
Thank Goodness
Their Adventure
Was over with - For Today

The White Tree
March 28, 2010

I happened to open up
The back door of the
dormitory
And to my surprise
Across the field
I beheld
A beautiful white tree!
The whole tree
Was in bloom
With little bunches of white
flowers
That almost touched the
ground
In the sunlight
It was really something to
behold
In all its
White Glory!

P.S.
Today - March 28, 2010
Shortly after finishing this
poem
The White Tree
It came to me
That I have now
Been writing poetry
For 25 years
I can hardly believe it!!!

Thank You - My Beautiful
God
For this Precious Gift!

A Simple Joy
August 1, 2010

I looked out
The kitchen window
And to my delight
I saw
A beautiful morning dove
Very busy
Finding breakfast

I stood there watching
For several minutes
As this beautiful dove
Hopped about
Here and there
Then I turned away
To get busy
Getting my breakfast

Untitled

Some days later
I happened to look out the kitchen window
And to my surprise
I saw
Four beautiful morning doves
Getting their breakfast

Sister Theresa Maria
Was nearby
So I showed them to her
When she saw them
Her face
Was filled with delight
And her smile
Became like sunshine
As we both
Paused a moment
To enjoy
This Simple Joy

The Bird and the Chipmunk
June 27, 2007

Looked out the window
While I was passing down the hall
Saw a bird hopping about
Behind a chipmunk
Trying to make him move
The chipmunk would go forward a little and stop
Then the bird would hop closer

Until he moved again
Finally
The chipmunk got tired
Turned around and chased
the bird
Who hopped fast
Instead of flying off
However
He came to his senses
And finally flew up and
away

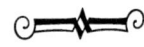

June 28, 2007

This morning
As I stood at the top
Of the back stairs
I saw another bird
On the side walk
And then Mr. Chipmunk
came along
The bird minded his
business
And the chipmunk kept to
his
There was no glash!
I guess they had
An Understanding!

Sweet Lady of the Sacristy
July 25, 2010

I don't' know
Where it came from
But on a slim wall shelf
In the Sacristy
I found
A statue of Our Lady
That has
A very sweet
And a very gentle
countenance
Her garment is white
And there is
A gold trimming
Around her neck
Her sleeves
And around the bottom
There is a long, flowing
Light blue cloak
Over it
And she is standing
Upon the world
Which is painted
In light green
Her hands are folded
And her fingers
Are inter-locked

All except one forefinger
Which has a special place
At the top of the rest
Her hair is light-brown
Her eyes
Are looking gently
downward
And there is a little red
Upon her lips
That express
The sweetest smile

I have enjoyed
Having her so much
As I go about my work
In the Sacristy
I often glance up at her
Or say a little prayer
Glad of her company
One thing
I find most unusual
Whenever I arrange flowers
For the Sanctuary
I try to have
One or two left
So that I can put them
In a little vase
For her
When I do
Long after the others are
thrown away
They just

Last and Last and Last!

The Pieta
July 25, 2010

There is a small
Pieta statue
By the Sacristy hall
As I go to and fro
I like to make
Some little Act of love
To show Our Lord
And Our Sorrowful Mother
That I really do love and
care for them
And truly Thank them
For all they have done for
me
And all generations

I seldom
Put a little vase of flowers
here
But I have noticed
When I do
It is like the ones by
The Sweet Lady in the
Sacristy
They seem
To last and last!

I wonder
Is Our Sorrowful Mother
And the Sweet Lady of the Sacristy
Performing
A real little miracle here
With their little bouquets

⁌━◆━⁍

April 3, 2011

I arranged
Two small vases
Of flowers
For Latarae Sunday
The Rose Sunday
During Lent
I put one
On each side
Of the Tabernacle
And they looked lovely

Later
I happened to notice
That one of them
Needed
A little something more
As soon as I could
I took
A small piece of baby's breath
That I had left over
And I inserted it
In the bouquet
What a difference
It made!

Then
I thought about
How sometimes
We think
The little things
We do
Do not really matter
Do not make a difference
Oftentimes
The little prayer
We send up so fervently
Each day for someone
Or some special intention
Or some special world event
Seems to fail
To help that someone
To help that Special Intention
And to help that world event
Let us not become discouraged
Because
We may be making
A very beautiful difference

and
A very significant difference
before
The Eyes of God

The Unexpected Gift
July 12, 2010

I had several rosaries
That I wanted
A medal of Our Lady
Attached to
These medals were
Of Our Lady of Medjugorie
That someone had given us
And the rosaries
Were made here
By some of our Sisters

These rosaries
Were very special to me
Because Mrs. Bruyere's
daughter Sarah
Had been ever so kind
And taken them with her
On her Pilgrimage to
Medjugorie
She had a Priest over there
To bless them
And also took them about
To some of their holy places
I was so grateful to God
And to Our Lady
And to Sarah

As Sister Josefa
Attached the medals
I spoke of wanting a medal
Of Holy Father
St. Frances de Sales
And of Holy Mother
St. Jane de Chantel
For my very special red
rosary
That I got
From the Vatican Gift Shop
When I went to Rome
Many years ago
And before I entered
And it had been blessed
By Pope Paul VI
To My Great Surprise and
Delight
She had several
And was glad to give me one
Which she soon attached
To my special red rosary

How happy I was
Over this
Most Unexpected Gift!

Rose of Sharon
July 4, 2007

Looked out the window
This morn
And saw
The Rose of Sharon bush
In bloom
There were a number
Of rose-colored blossoms
And a number of white ones
With rose-colored centers
They looked truly beautiful

As I admired them
It brought to mind
A Baptist Church in
Alexandria
That was named
Rose of Sharon
And it brought back the memory
Of when my Dear Mother
Loved to go to Church
And would occasionally go there
On visits
When the Interstate went thru
It almost swept it away
But the people prevailed
And with God's help
Saved It!

I pray
That it will always be
As beautiful as this flower
And be a beacon of Christ
And a little oasis
To all who travel by its way
On this busy thoroughfare

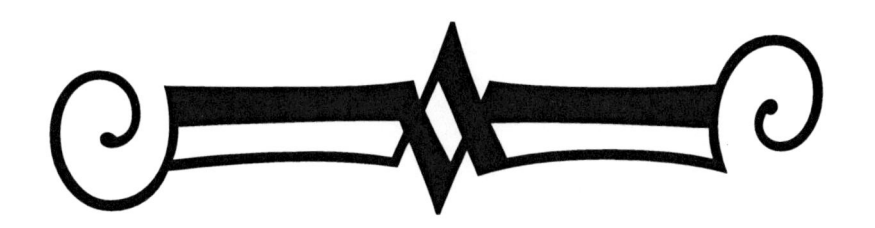

Atlanta's Special Child

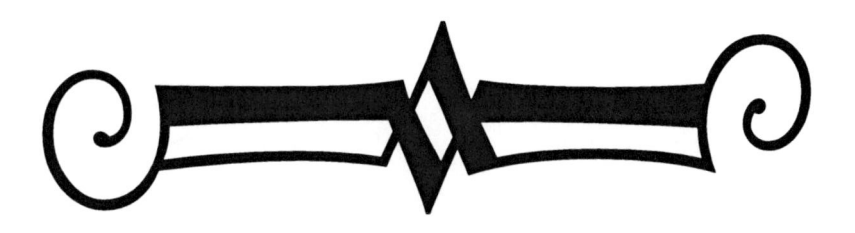

My Bonnie Blue

How you lighted up my heart
the first moment I looked at you.
You were so tiny, delicate, and sweet.
Your eyes were so beautiful
capturing the deepest blue of the sea
And your hair shone as gloriously as the sun.

I wanted to give you the best of everything -
clothes, home, and the best education
that money could buy.
I wanted you to see the world
and learn of its people and cultures.
I even changed my way of life
so that only a good reputation would fall upon you.
Nothing was too good for my Bonnie Blue.

And then one day without warning
God came
and within an instant
My Bonnie Blue was gone

GONE WITH THE WIND

Little girl in the movie Gone With The Wind
As I saw her through Rhett Butler's eyes

Part Nine

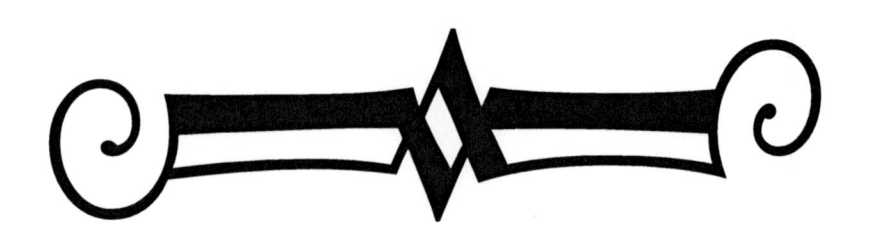

The Perfect Gift

Dedicated
To
The Sacred Heart of Jesus

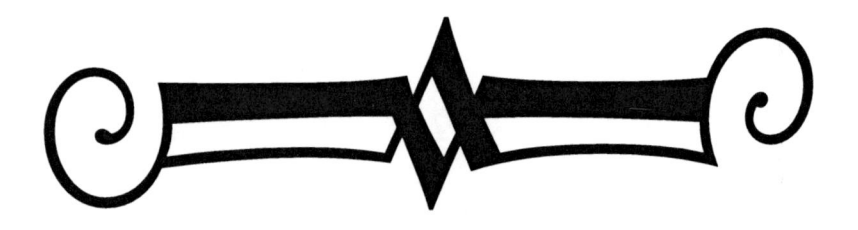

The Perfect Gift
February 13, 2011

Tomorrow
Will be
Valentine's Day
And I thought
What can I give
My Heart
He has
Everything
There is nothing
Absolutely Nothing
That He needs

Come
Sweet Holy Spirit
Come
And let me know
The Perfect Gift
That I can give
My Heart
The One
Who has Every thing

Then this came to me

O My Heart
Let me give you
My hands willingly

To carry out
The Mission
You have given me

My feet
That they may
Take me about
To carry out this work

Let me
Give you my eyes
To look about
To see
What needs to be done
To help my Fellow man
To help
Those close to me

Let me
Give you my mind
That it may be
Enlightened
With the Gifts
Of your Holy Spirit
That it may serve you
And all my Fellow men
Most effectively

Let me
Give you my speech
That I may be
A witness to you

On my pilgrimage
Thru this world
Speaking
Only the words
You want me to speak
And speaking them
To the ones
That you desire
That you place
Along my path

Now
Let me
Give you my will
That you may
Conform it to thine
Because
In your will
The very Best
Is accomplished

Most of all
I give you
My heart
Which is
Overflowing
With love for you
So deep
I cannot express it
But I will say
In giving you
My heart

I am giving you
My life
And my whole being
Filled with
A desire beyond
To please you
Each and every moment
Of my life
Each and every breath
That I take

May I
Forever be yours
And you
Forever be mine

O My Precious! Precious!
Sacred Heart of Jesus

⚜

Sweet Holy Spirit
I just want to say
Thank you
For answering my prayer
And answering it
Ever so quickly
May
My Precious Sacred Heart
Be ever so pleased
With this
Valentine's Day Gift

S. Green.
Photo taken 2011, during My Time in Atlanta.

To order for resale, contact:

Our Written Lives
book publishing services
www.owlofhope.com

CPSIA information can be obtained
at www.ICGtesting.com
Printed in the USA
FFOW05n1251300914